# HANGAR TALES
# & WAR STORIES
## THE HUMOR &
## ADVENTURE OF FLYING

# HANGAR TALES
# & WAR STORIES
## THE HUMOR &
## ADVENTURE OF FLYING

### BY JEFF W. GRIFFIN
### ILLUSTRATED BY JOHN T. JENSON

**TAB** TAB BOOKS Inc.

BLUE RIDGE SUMMIT, PA 17214

## Other TAB Books by the Author

No. 2255    *Passing Your Instrument Pilot's Written Exam*
No. 2273    *Cold Weather Flying*
No. 2293    *Instrument Flying*
No. 2318    *How to Become a Flight Engineer*
No. 2331    *Pilot's Guide to Weather Forecasting*
No. 2345    *Foundations of Flying*

FIRST EDITION

FIRST PRINTING

Library of Congress Cataloging in Publication Data

Griffin, Jeff.
    Hangar tales and war stories.

    Includes index.
    1. Aeronautics—Miscellanea. I. Title.
TL546.7.G75   1984      629.13'09      84-8901
ISBN 0-8306-2355-8 (pbk.)

Cover illustration by John T. Jenson.

*Dedicated to the memory of Dale Waldo, a truly great friend.*

# Contents

# Introduction

A flying career has many facets; yet every career has a common thread. They all start with desire. From this desire comes the students who, in a myriad of airplanes, go forth into a world that brings them in touch with many different emotions. Almost every student will, at some time in his or her training, experience fear, confusion, pleasure, and a sense of accomplishment.

Beyond that each other career diverges from the rest. Naturally, there are similarities, but they are few except when at some point two more careers cross. The relationships that develop in the cockpit between flight crew members are good examples. Into a crew relationship come all the personal experiences of the individuals, and in some instances new experiences are contrived or develop as fate deals them. It is from such personal experiences and relationships that these stories come to you.

Hangar flying, as it is sometimes called, has been a part of the aviation experience since Otto Lillienthal first flew his gliders. Hangar tales were swapped between the boys that flew in the Lafayette Escadrille, and between the good ol' boys at the grass airports somewhere in Texas. The fact is that hangar flying is entertaining and educational, but most of all it marks a fellowship.

To those new to aviation the term "war story" may need to be defined. Whenever pilots exchange tales of near mishaps with one another, that is a war story. Generally, war stories have nothing to do with war or warbirds, though some do.

Hangar tales are a little different from war stories. Generally, these stories are true in their origin but have been embellished through their retelling over the years. The exaggerations and embellishments are what make the stories worth reading. The reader can be assured that *something like that* happened *somewhere* at *sometime*.

The names of the characters in this book have been changed to protect the guilty. Only they know what lies they and I have perpetrated in the interest of entertaining reading. In many ways they should be thankful that I have left out the sordid details of their escapades. Regretfully, I had to leave as many stories out of this book as I put in. The sort of stories I allude to are those about flight crews found in compromising situations. The captain who occasionally flies naked or runs down the empty aisles of a plane in just his boots during a ferry flight, to the embarassment of the flight attendants, are good examples.

Yes, these things have happened and will happen. Anecdotes are exchanged almost daily. Some are worth printing and many others are not. In this book I hope you will find some humor, some tense situations, and a little romance. The book is, I believe, a cross section of the experiences of pilots as they pursue their careers. It is also a good way to spend a stormy night when no one in his right mind wants to be flying against the elements.

An old sign at the grass airport sums up the long history of war stories and hangar tales that some airports have. It looks like this:

| | | |
|---|---|---|
| Maintenance: | | $24.00/hr. |
| C-150 | : | $18.00/hr. |
| C-172 | : | $24.00/hr. |
| Instruction | : | $ 7.00/hr. |
| Hangar Flying Free | | |

# Where There's Smoke . . .
## (There's a Joke)

It's a baptism of fire whenever a new flight attendant takes on the job of catering in the sky. Some flight deck crews are relentless in their practical jokes with the new girls.

On one such occasion, Big Bob Turner, as he is known, fell heir to one country bumpkin during her first week of flight duty with the airline. We'll call this gal "Country Nelda." She was fresh off the farm in southwestern Oklahoma and had gotten married right out of high school. For the most part, a trip to the county seat was as far as she had been. On the positive side, she was serious about her job and knew all about her airplane and duties. Unfortunately, this was the trait that big Bob could best exploit.

The airplane that the crew was assigned to fly was a 30-seat arrangement, a Shorts SD 3-30 to be exact. It looks like a boxcar, but is very comfortable and has a warning system for every malfunction known to man. For each of those warnings there is a corresponding test. For example, the forward and aft baggage compartments contain smoke detectors which, if triggered, will activate a light on the annunciator panel. The test switch for the smoke lights is on the right cockpit wall by the first officer. It is possible for the first officer to trigger the light very inconspicuously. The reason this is so easy is because there are two doors to the cockpit, one behind each pilot. Thus, if the flight attendant were summoned by the Captain, she would come to his side, leaving the copilot to manipulate the switches unnoticed. This is precisely what the flight crew did.

Flashing the flight attendant to pick up the interphone, Captain Turner made this request: "Nelda could you come up here for a minute, please? We have a little problem and could use your assistance."

"I'll be right there," she said, and hung up the phone.

Up on the flight deck, the crew were grinning at each other like a couple of monkeys. When the light from the cabin splashed into the cockpit from behind, the boys were just putting on their straight faces.

Nelda was all ears to hear the details of the problem. "Nelda," the Captain began, "we've been gettin' an intermittent smoke light from the aft baggage compartment. Now, what I suspect is that the guys who load the bags on the airplane left the light on when they were finished. It's just possible that it's gettin' real hot back there and causing that little plastic shade around the light bulb to smolder."

About that time the copilot flipped the test switch and the smoke aft light came on. "Did you see that?" The captain looked back over his shoulder to Nelda.

"Boy, I sure did. What do you want me to do? You want me to fire that fire extinguisher through that little hole in the back?" Nelda indeed knew her aircraft, but the captain wanted to keep things drawn out and unobtrusive to the passengers.

"No, Nelda, what we need first is to determine if there is indeed a problem. Go back there and peep through that fire extinguisher port and check if the light is on." The captain gave the order in his most honest-sounding voice. All the while, he knew she would never see a thing due to a little cap on the back side that is to be knocked away by inserting a fire extinguisher.

The door slid closed. The guys slapped their knees, but held back the laughter for fear Nelda would hear it as she walked away. She'd fallen for the story. As she walked towards the rear of the airplane the trim changed, so the captain knew when she was at the rear. Winking at his first officer and gesturing his head toward the door, the two slid their individual doors open to see what Nelda was doing. There she was, leaning against the rear bulkhead, peering into that little fire extinguisher port. They quickly closed the doors and waited for her to come back and report.

"Captain, I can't see a thing through that little hole. Are you sure I'm supposed to see through that little thing?" Her country twang was just about enough to drive the crew to laughter, but Big Bob kept his composure.

"Of course you can see through that thing. For crying out loud, I've looked through that thing lots of times, but the light may be out. If it is, you won't be able to see a thing." He stopped for a moment and thought: then, to his first officer's surprise, made a ludicrous request. "Nelda, we really have no way to know if this smoke detection system is working properly. What we need you to do now is to go back there and sniff that little hole and see if you can catch a whiff of smoke. Could you do that for us?" Big Bob let out a deep breath as he finished that one. What a whopper!

"Damn, Bob," the first officer let out an exclamation of disbelief. "I can't believe you said that and kept a straight face."

2

"Shhhh." The captain put his finger to his lips. "Let's see if she does it."

Sliding the doors open again, the crew became delighted. There, up against the bulkhead at the rear, was Country Nelda, sniffing away at that little hole—a ridiculous sight, embellished by the puzzled look on several passengers' faces.

"Geez, Bob, she's going for this thing all the way," the first officer reported. "I wonder what she's gonna say this time."

About that time the captain's cockpit door slid open. "Bob, I can't smell a thing through that little hole." It was apparent that Country Nelda was depressed.

"Well, Nelda, maybe we don't have a fire. We're just about to land, so just check it again before we touch down. If you detect *anything,* let us know. Okay?" Captain Bob was trying to let her down easy, but it didn't work.

After doing the shutdown checklist at the arrival gate, Big Bob went to the rear of the plane to exit through the rear door and check the refueling. Nelda was at the rear saying goodbye to the last passenger getting off. She grabbed Bob by the sleeve. "The ramp agents are unloading the bags right now, aren't they?" she asked.

"Yeah, they sure are." Captain Turner was unconcerned about the question. In his mind the whole shtick was over, but Nelda persisted.

"Then that light in the rear compartment should be on, shouldn't it?" Country Nelda was using a little deductive reasoning.

"Well sure, I would think it would be on," said Bob, completely undisturbed.

But Country Nelda wanted to know for sure. "Bob, would you look through that little hole and see if you can see the light?"

The captain leaned against the bulkhead and squinted through the hole. Then he straightened up and started for the door.

"Well, did you see it?" Nelda demanded.

Big Bob, knowing that he hadn't seen a thing through the hole, said, "Sure Nelda, the light's on."

Now, in the captain's mind, this is where the story would end. He couldn't believe that she hadn't caught on to the gag yet. Soon, though, his first officer followed him outside and called him over to the side.

"Bob, what did you just tell Nelda? She's in there crying her eyes out." The copilot was genuinely concerned.

Bob quickly explained she had asked him to look through the hole and that he had lied about seeing the light.

"Well, you'd better go back inside and set her straight, Bob," the copilot requested. "She's really torn up."

As Bob entered the plane, Nelda was sitting there crying. She looked up at him and in a completely innocent country voice said, "I just can't see anything or smell anything through that hole, Bob. Do you think I should get my eyes and my nose checked?"

"Your nose checked?" Bob's brain was convulsing with laughter, but he kept a straight face. "You mean that you didn't get the 'Burnt Weenie Test' before you went on the line?" He said it as if he were aghast.

"No sir." Nelda was disappointed that she missed something.

"Well then, we'll just have to certify you on this next flight." Bob had that twinkle in his eye and he was off and running again.

The first officer followed him back to the cockpit, just shaking his head at the whole thing.

# The Race

Rio Airways is a large commuter airline in central Texas. They are large because they extend quite a ways to the east into Arkansas, Tennessee, and Mississippi. Because the company is so gregarious, they have always been a strong competitor to my own airline, which is Metro. Although the two companies are very different in route structure, we do share one route. That route is from Wichita Falls, Texas, into the Dallas-Fort Worth Regional Airport. It is normal for both airlines to spy on each other in order to determine what each others' departure times will be during the following schedule change. The result is that the departure times are usually the same. This made for some very good racing starts and at least on unique finish.

Before the Air Traffic Controllers' strike in late 1981, it was common for both carriers to be released from Wichita Falls at about the same time. One flight would follow the other by only the amount of time that it took for the first plane to clear the runway on its crosswind turn.

On a warm day in May the stage was set for a classic match of airplane and crews. Rio and Metro at this time were both operating identical equipment, de Havilland Twin Otters. On this particular day even the ground crews were scurrying around, trying to get their respective company's airplane loaded with baggage and passengers first. As luck would have it, Rio had their airplane out of the blocks first. Well, somebody has to go first, but sometimes we could work this to our advantage—as we did this day.

We taxied out right on Rio's heels, winding around the airport's taxiways to the runway. As we taxied, my copilot, Tom Muzinich, and I worked on strategy, which went something like this: Since both of the airplanes were very much alike, the performance would be the same. Rio was going first. That meant that we would be able to select the best altitude. Ordinarily, the higher the altitude, the better, due to the potential energy that we would store, though we would have to climb for a longer period of time and our groundspeed during the climb would be less than

that at cruise. A sort of compromise was necessary.

On this particular day Rio chose to stop their climb at 7,500 feet. We were only two or three minutes behind them. When their climb halted, their groundspeed was going to increase, and if we were to continue to 9,500 feet, they would begin to stretch out their lead during that time. In order to minimize this effect I put the airplane in a cruise-climb configuration. There were about 50 or 60 miles ahead before Rio would begin their descent into DFW airport. If we hit our target altitude of 9,500 feet by that time or before, we could win the race.

Rio was stretching their lead, just as we had expected, but we had our 9,500 feet in the bag only halfway to the descent point. Our higher true airspeed at 9,500 begin to close the gap somewhat, a fact I hadn't even considered until now. We were in good position to pounce down on Rio. Once they began their descent we would have them where we wanted them. You see, since we had an extra 2,000 feet of altitude to play with, we could keep the airplane up against redline speed for a longer period of time. That should be enough to close the gap between us and more than likely overtake them.

Then something happened that altered our plan of attack. The upper levels of the Terminal Control Area began to get in the way. Rio was already lower and I don't believe they knew how close we were. Believing that they had already won the daily race by being first to leave the terminal, their pace was a great deal more relaxed than ours. However, the overhanging layers of the TCA "wedding cake" had forced us just about three or four hundred feet above Rio.

Rio was the first to call in to Regional approach and that blew our cover. Upon his call-in the controller called us as three o'clock traffic less than a mile, same direction, same speed. Uh-oh, the real race for the airport was on.

Now, there aren't too many things a pilot can do to make a Twin Otter go faster. One, he can bring the power to redline limits and two, he can bring the propeller rpm up to 86 percent from the normal 76 percent. The Rio captain did this and so did we. Then we called-in and were issued our neighboring traffic— Rio.

There is something you should know. In those days, there was a prescribed arrival route for VFR flights such as Rio and Metro. In fact, it was designed for the use of both airlines. This meant that no matter what, we were destined to fly next to each other all the way to the airport. You should also know that there are two approach sectors, each under the watchful eye of a different controller. There is an outlying sector and a smaller one near the airport where each aircraft gets final sequencing and a runway assignment. The first approach controller could have split us up and made it easy for the following sequencing controller, but he was enjoying the race as much as we were. He passed the buck.

Rio was hanging onto us like a leech. Side by side we whistled towards the airport. It was going to be a standoff until the controller made a decision for runway assignment. He was in an unenviable position, for as we were handed off to him it was readily apparent that neither one of us was giving an inch in our airborne position.

A final consideration was now introduced into the race. We almost always raced just to the airport and the first one to land was considered the winner, but that wouldn't be enough today. Landing on the north-south runway on the west side of the airport and terminal complex meant an extra 10-minute taxi to the gate. We had to get the runway on the east side to win.

It was decision time for the controller. He had waited until almost too late to see if one of us was going to slow down and let the other in. Neither of us did. It was then that he did something very unexpected. He threw the ball back in our court.

"Rio 670 and Metro 1018. One of you is going to have to go to 35 left and one of you is going to have to go to 35 right. What's it going to be?" he flipped the question nonchalantly.

"Uh-oh," I thought. "Why, that's downright dastardly." That's when I noticed the radio silence: *Rio hadn't said a thing—yet.* So, in my deepest, most different voice, I keyed the mike and said, "Approach, why don't you let old Metro go on over to the east side?"

"Well, thank you Rio. Metro, you're first for 35 right, and Rio you are number one for 35 left. Contact tower. . ." The din of our laughter drowned out the rest of his transmission.

Now, I admit that this was dirty pool, but how sweet the victory as we waved at Rio when they taxied in 10 minutes later.

And Rio? Well, they got even on another night.

# The Flasher

Charlie Ruggles was out mowing his yard. When he finished the last strip, he was dying to go inside and have a beer. As he hit the door, the phone began ringing. It was the dispatcher from Charlie's company, Texas International Airways. All hopes for a cool beer quickly died as the situation developed.

"Charlie, this is Bill down at dispatch. Boy, am I glad I got a hold of you! We need a pilot to take a trip up to Dallas and Fort Worth."

By this time Charlie was shaking his head. "But Bill, this is my day off," he began to plead his case.

The dispatcher sighed, then apologized. "Charlie, the scheduled crew ran out of duty time and you are the only one we can find to fly the trip." The dispatcher was doing some fast talking.

Thinking fast, Charlie pulled his ace out of the hole. At least he *thought* it was a winning card: "Bill, I don't even have a uniform. Mine is in the cleaners." He waited to see what they would say about *that*.

"At this point, Charlie, it's a moot point. We have to have you. Just show up like you are." The dispatcher was just trying to get the job done.

Charlie looked down at himself. Just in from mowing the yard he had on a sweaty, dirty, white T-shirt, a pair of khaki bermuda shorts, and grass-stained tennis shoes. He looked a sight and he knew it. He was just about to say something when the dispatcher broke in.

"Charlie, are you still there?" The dispatcher was getting antsy.

"Well, yeah." Charlie was dazed that his ace-in-the-hole hadn't worked.

"Well, the flight leaves in 20 minutes. Get out here right away." The dispatcher hung up the phone.

Now, Charlie thought about the situation and then grinned to himself. This was, in effect, a license to steal. He began to relish the idea of flying up to Fort Worth in his bermudas. When

he arrived at the airport, the dispatchers sneaked him onto the airplane ahead of the passengers. Charlie was beginning to enjoy this new sort of freedom—free from a suit and tie, that is.

In the days that this story happened, things were much different than they are today. Texas International was flying Convair 600s as their largest airplane. Also, the route that Charlie was to fly that day was taking him from Houston Hobby Airport to the Greater Southwest Airport between Fort Worth and Dallas, a route that is no longer in existence. Moreover, the FAA Accident Inspection and Air Carrier Divisions were located on the field at Greater Southwest Airport—a fact that gave Charlie some problems later.

Charlie was enjoying the flight. He had his grass-stained tennis shoes propped up on the flight panel and delicately held the yoke in his left hand. It was a smooth flight right up to the touchdown, and then all hell broke loose. As the nosewheel touched the runway, it clipped a large stovebolt that had been dropped on the runway by a mowing machine. The tire flipped the bolt into the right propeller, breaking off a chunk about a foot long. The prop tip then became a missile launching itself into the belly of the fuselage, severing control cables and causing the left engine to slam into full reverse.

At this point Charlie had his hands full. The right engine was shaking itself apart and the left engine wanted to go the other direction. An emergency shutdown was necessary for both engines and the crew pursued that action quickly. Keeping the airplane on the runway took a master's touch and Charlie had it. As the airplane rolled to a stop, the flight attendant began an emergency evacuation and had the passengers off in a flash.

With the airplane dead on the runway and the passengers out and standing around the plane, Charlie had time to think about things to come. He remembered the FAA and knew they would be out to the airplane very soon. He looked down at his clothes and headed for a ramp agent who had come out on a baggage tug to see if he could help.

Charlie walked up to him and explained, "The FAA will be here any minute. Can you get me something to put over these clothes. I'm afraid what the passengers and the FAA might think."

The ramp agent was back in a minute or two with a raincoat that had "Texas International" stenciled in big letters on the back. Charlie quickly donned it as the FAA showed up and began to go over the airplane. He stole back into the crowd and hoped that the FAA wouldn't notice him.

The FAA pored over the airplane, sticking their heads in every orifice like a doctor giving an examination. Somewhere during that time it began to dawn on them that they had not yet seen the captain of the flight. One of the inspectors took it upon himself to find him. It turned out to be an inspector who had given Charlie several check rides in the past. As the inspector descended the stairs from the airplane, he looked out over the crowd of passengers still milling around and awaiting further transportation. Towards the back he spotted a familiar face—Charlie's.

The inspector made his way through the crowd towards Charlie. As he came close enough to see him from head to toe he stopped. There stood Charlie looking like a Central Park deviate, his hairy legs jutting from under the yellow raincoat and down into his grass-stained tennis shoes.

The inspector began to shake his head slowly as he began to speak to Charlie: "Well, Captain Ruggles, you've done it this time. We've gone over the airplane, at least preliminarily, and find that this incident has in no way tainted your flying career.

"On the other hand, Captain, we may have you on a morals charge."

Charlie just smiled sheepishly and shrugged. What else could he do?

# The Building Block

The DC-3 was droning monotonously towards Corpus Christi as it bobbed daintily on the late evening air currents. As the day's light faded, the red lights illuminating the instrument panel became more noticeable. Captain Roger Ferguson and his copilot, Gary London, were finishing their lunches and talking idly. In the cabin, Sandra Martin was finishing up her initial rounds of her beverage service. It was her first day with the airline, at least flying a regular route. She was very conscientious about her new position, as all new flight attendants are. It was late fall, 1959, and Trans Texas Airways was struggling to stay competitive with Delta and Eastern in the Texas market. The success of the airline (which one day would grow into Texas International) was resting fairly on its aircrews. Yet often there was time to play.

Roger and Gary had flown together often over the past few years. They were friends in and out of the cockpit. Roger was known as the instigator and Gary was the collaborator. As Roger folded his brown lunch bag and put it into his flight bag, Gary caught a glimpse of Roger's thoughtful look. Something was up. Gary thought that Roger was probably contemplating one of his practical jokes. He hoped that he would not be the intended target, then let the thought go.

From Roger's point of view, it was part of his job to keep crew morale up in these early days of the airlines. Besides, he loved to break in a new stewardess. He already had a plan in mind as he reached into his flight case. From within he drew a kid's building block—the kind that's made of wood and has a letter on each side. He rolled the perfect cube over several times in his hand, examining it, thinking. Gary watched him out of the corner of his eye and wondered what he was thinking.

Soon Roger reached back into his flight kit and brought out a ball of string. He motioned with an extended thumb over his shoulder. It became instantly clear to Gary that they were about to perpetrate something obnoxious on Sandra.

"Where in the world do you get all that stuff you find in your

flight kit?" Gary was puzzled and amazed at the same time.

"Oh, I just pick up stuff here and there. You never know when you might find a use for something."

"Well, what are you gonna do with that?"

"You'll see very shortly." With that, Roger turned his attention back to the building block. He began to wrap the string around the block as if he were wrapping a parcel. Biting the string off, he tied the ends and attached the loose end of the string on the ball to the block. It looked like a tiny box kite, but it would never fly.

Gary was anxious with anticipation of Roger's plan, but he kept his mouth shut. Roger slipped his cockpit window open just enough for the block. Gary chuckled to himself as it became apparent what Roger was going to do.

"Ooh, this is gonna be good!" Gary could no longer hide his enthusiasm for the plan.

Roger stuffed the building block through the window and slid it almost closed. There was just enough room left to feed the string out the crack. As Roger let the string out slowly, the block began to move backward in the slipstream. After a few feet of string had been let out, the block began to knock against the fuselage. It was doing just what Roger had hoped it would do.

Meanwhile, Sandra was warming up the passengers' coffee with refills. As she reached across an aisle seat to an older gentleman sitting by the window to refill his cup, she heard the knocking outside. At first she chose to ignore it and go on about her duties, but then it became obvious that the passenger had heard it too. This was indeed a foreign sound and perhaps the crew should be informed. She walked quickly back to her galley station and put the coffeepot on the warmer. Wiping her hands, she walked briskly up the aisle towards the cockpit door.

Gary was flying the plane on this leg and he could feel the center of gravity change. "Roger she's coming." The crew shot evil smiles at each other.

As Sandra opened the door, the light from the cabin poured into the darkened cockpit. Both pilots were looking straight ahead so as not to arouse her suspicions nor cause each other to laugh.

"Captain, someone is trying to get in!" The absurdity of the statement almost choked the flight crew.

"Well," sighed Roger, "I guess you can let them in, but tell them I don't think their bags made it."

At that moment it became extremely hard for Sandra to swallow her own credulity. Red-faced, she spun on her heel and retreated to the sound of the pilots' howls and knee slaps.

# The Virgin Test Light

This story comes from Captain Maynard (Ret.) of National Airlines. Like the rest of the stories in this book, some of the most amusing anecdotes are true to the core. Incidents like this one go on every day, but it takes a good storyteller to bring some of them to life. Here's the story as I first heard it.

The end of another day was close at hand. The 727 had just about completed its appointed rounds with one instrument approach to go. The flight crew ran the before-landing checklist and briefed one another on the upcoming instrument descent and approach. In the midst of all this Captain Maynard pushed the test light switch for the marker beacon lights. As he was doing this, one of the flight attendants came through the cockpit door. Seeing the lights come on aroused her curiosity. Even though she was an experienced hand, she was like most flight attendants, who spend very little time up front where they can notice much of anything.

"Captain, what are those lights that just came on and then went off?" She was asking a legitimate question. However, as most pilots are wont to do, he turned it into a situation to pull a gag. Checking to see if she had even an inkling of what they might be, he probed, "You've never seen those before?"

"No sir, I can't say that I have ever seen them before," she answered quite matter-of-factly.

"Well, Freda, that is the Virgin Test Light system," he answered with a straight face, but there was a twinkle in his eye. "Look, if you press this button right here, the system will check your virginity. If the lights illuminate, it means your virginity is intact. Go ahead and try it."

Freda looked at him apprehensively and then reached down and pushed the test switch. All the lights on the marker beacon panel lit up.

"Well, there it is, Freda—proof positive that you're still a virgin," The Captain spoke as if he was proud of his test machine.

"Captain, I hate to tell you . . ." She paused to let the cockpit fill with anticipation. ". . . but your equipment is broken. And as quickly as she had come, she was gone.

# The Toilet Motor Overheat

Since stewardesses first came on the airline scene they have been the butt of flight crew practical jokes. The reason for this is twofold. First, every new girl wants to do her best as she begins her new career. This leads to a certain amount of gullibility. Secondly, most stewardesses and flight attendants have no technical knowledge of airplanes in general and thus have to trust the flight crews for warnings that a particular item is not functioning as it should. The flight crews have always known this and use it to their advantage to pull off certain practical jokes.

If it seems there are a large number of flight attendant tales in this book, your observation is correct. I suppose the reason for this is that flying, for the most part, is more fun than terrifying on most given days. It is flavor that most pilots savor. Because of this one truth, pilots tend to stir up a little mischief to keep the day from passing too slowly.

It's unfortunate but true that some flight attendants are more naive than others. Country Nelda, one of the favorite targets, really got raked over the coals during the first few weeks she was on the job. Nelda believed that the airplanes that airlines fly have a warning system or light for every item or system on the airplane. Although they *are* quite well equipped, to assume that the toilet motor has an overheat warning in the cockpit is just a bit much. Nonetheless, this is exactly what Big Bob Turner intended to perpetrate on Nelda.

Bob Turner was known as an excellent pilot and one of the most fun captains to fly with. Most copilots would finish the month with him and realize they had learned a great deal. They would know more about flying, and they would *certainly* know more about the art of practical joking. Most of all, they would know how relentless to Country Nelda Big Bob could be. In fact, she almost quit after this particular episode.

Bob looked over at his copilot. He flipped the emergency light switch off and the red pilot light came on. "Do you think ol' Nelda would believe that this is a toilet motor overheat light?"

Jim Spencer was filling the right seat. "You know Nelda. If you told her we had ejection seats she'd believe it," he said, matter-of-factly.

"Well, let's call her up front and tell her we have a problem." Big Bob had a twinkle in his eye. He reached over and punched the flight attendant call button. Country Nelda picked up the interphone. "Nelda, we have a little problem that we need your help with. Could you come up here for just a minute?"

Nelda arrived in just a few seconds and was eager to help as always. The captain spoke slowly and deliberately to make sure she understood: "Nelda, this light here is the toilet motor overheat light." He glanced at her quickly to see if she was buying the story. She was, so he continued.

"Now, this happens occasionally. The toilet motor sometimes won't shut off after a flush. What I need you to do is to go back there and check if the motor is still engaged. You might have to get down and listen for it," he added as she started to turn around to go and check.

Jim was about to laugh himself to tears after hearing his captain's spiel. They both turned around to watch Nelda check the toilet motor. She walked to the aft of the cabin, where the lavatory was located, and stuck her head right in, listening carefully.

When she came back to the cockpit, the crew was stonefaced as usual. In her country twang she confessed, "I listened real good and I didn't hear nothin'."

"Well, the light has gone out now. I'll call you if it goes on again." The captain told her this so as not to make too much of the situation all at once. He was figuring that if he waited a few minutes and then called her again she would be convinced that there was a real problem with the toilet.

"Okay," she twanged. "Just let me know if I need to do somethin'."

"Jim looked a little puzzled and even a little disappointed that the captain had stopped the joke so soon, so Bob let him in on the plan. Several minutes went by and the crew rang for Nelda again.

"That doggone light is on again, Nelda. I'm afraid we have a real problem with that toilet." Jim was doing his part now to add credence to the whole scam.

"I don't really see what I can do with it. Besides, it don't sound like it's a runnin' to me."

"You can believe that it's running if this light is on," said Jim.

At that point the captain broke in with a suggestion: "I believe we can bring down the temperature of the motor if you will flush a couple buckets of ice down the toilet. The light should go off right away."

Country Nelda looked at him a little quizzically, then she was gone. Bob and Jim watched her through the cockpit doors. As she went to the galley to get a bucket of ice, Jim commented, "Geez, this is better than the smoke light gag!"

Nelda got a bucket of ice from the galley and went into the lavatory. The pilots could see her bend over and start the toilet flushing. She looked up and saw them. Both of them motioned to her that the light hadn't gone out yet. Nelda shrugged and went back to the galley to get another bucket of ice.

As she went into the lavatory the second time, a passenger got up to go back and use the facility. He was a tall man decked out in a western suit, and presumably from Dallas, since that is where the plane began its flight.

Nelda was busy swishing her ice cubes down the john and did not notice the tall man looking over her shoulder. When she looked up and saw him standing over her she started to explain. He didn't give her a chance. He spoke in a way only a true Texas gentleman can:

"Ma'am, if that's the way you mix drinks on this airplane, would you cancel my order?"

Nelda finally realized the crew had put her up to the whole thing. She started for the cockpit. As she did, the boys shut their doors and bolted the lock. They could hear her trying to get in, but didn't want any part of her fury. When they got to the destination they both went out the emergency exit at the front of the plane while she said goodbye to the passengers at the rear of the plane. Cowards!

# 202 GW

The first time I saw her she was standing in the growing twilight of a Minneapolis sunset. Her prominent nose pointed skyward. The large "walking gear" some four feet under her belly looked like the black shoes that Minnie Mouse wears. Due to her taildragger configuration she seemed to sit back on her haunches. I'd like to call it a dainty pose, but it wasn't. She was just hunkered down there waiting for her cargo and another go at the elements of the night.

Pilots have known for a long time that the romance of flying is often wrapped up in the planes they fly. There have always been special planes: the *Spirit of St. Louis*, the Wright Brother's Flyer, and even 202 GW. *202 GW?* Well, maybe you haven't ever heard of 202 GW, but I have run across several comrades that fly with me at Metro Airlines that knew her well. You might say that these guys come from the same flying stock that I do. In my biased opinion, that makes them good pilots—the best. To take one of those crazy-looking Turbine Beech 18s across the country in the dead of night and into a skyful of thunderstorms takes skill. It also takes a great deal of luck.

When we recall our days of flying freight for the now defunct Great Western Airlines we all agree on three things: It was a horrible company to work for. The maintenance was none-existant. And 202 GW was the best plane that Great Western had.

The things that made 202 GW so special were her paint job and the nav package. As a general rule, freight airplanes are beat-up old relics that aren't good for anything else, but 202 GW had been revitalized. She began life as an ordinary Beech 18 with a short snubby nose and radial engines that coughed and spewed half-burned oil with the best of them. Then she got her Hamilton conversion, and with it two powerful PT6-20 turboprop engines and a stinger of a nose. The metamorphosis wasn't exactly that of a caterpillar changing into a beautiful butterfly; it was more like a tortoise changing into a hare. After the conversion she would true out at better than 200 knots—and that's *fast* for a Beech 18.

Two-Oh-Two's paint job was nice—not flamboyant, not pretty, just nice. At the same time it was also extraordinary, probably because she even had a paint job at all. The top of the nose was painted a flat black to guard against glare. I don't know why, because she hardly ever flew during the light of day, yet it was her most striking feature. The side had two thin stripes, one of gold and one of crimson. The twin vertical stabilizers and rudders were each painted with the gold, crimson, and black logo of the ariline. The whole effect was striking, especially in contrast to the other tired old dogs strewn around the ramp. It was for this reason that she made us feel elite. I mean, when we rolled onto the freight ramp at the crack of midnight, *we looked good*!

Outfitted with her new paint job and radios she was ready to take on the world. Her wings already had 9,000 or 10,000 hours of hard use and were relegated to making at least twice that much in the coming years. For freighters the hours come hard. Many routes completed at night are at the expense of putting the wings into thunderstorms as explosive as dynamite. Although anyone—even a freight pilot—will tell you not to fly into thunderstorms, the nightly victories of the freight world are won that way.

The Hamilton standard conversion for the Beech 18 was an effort to beef up tired old Beeches and allow the freight operators to haul more freight per flight. The reason for the stinger-like nose on the front was to compensate for the extra gross weight allowed in the main cargo area aft of the cockpit. The PT6 engines, you see, were quite a bit more powerful than the radials and would haul more weight aloft. The immediate trouble with this is that the wings were placed too far forward for the added allowable weight. In other words, the plane was tailheavy when loaded to maximum gross weight. Thus they added sheet metal on the front of the plane. It turned the classic lines of the Beech 18 into what I heard a Northwest Airlines pilot call "a real fancy bug smasher."

In addition to the two obvious additions to the Beech (the engines and the nose), there was also a hidden modification. It was referred to as a spar strap. Its purpose was to strengthen the main spar of the wings through the cabin/fuselage area. Now, all this is fine until you get to thinking that if a guy gets into a *real* bad storm and the wings get broke, all they'll do is to fold up like the wings of a Navy fighter on an aircraft carrier. Why the entire spar was not replaced is no mystery—cost. That one consideration made me wonder a lot of nights as we nursed 202

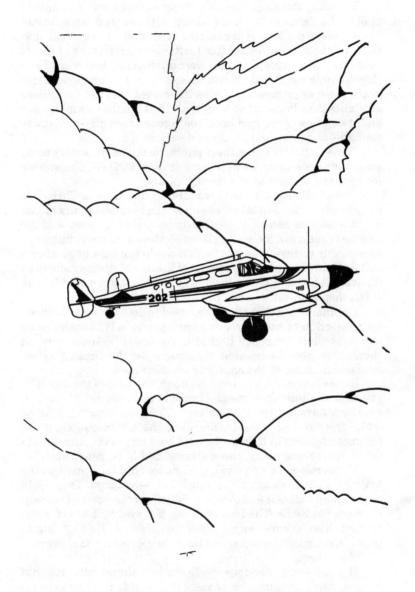

GW around the big ones just how many storms she had in her. Believe me, a glance in the logbook of any of those Turbine 18s would make a pilot wonder just how long his luck would hold out.

Probably the most amazing thing is that I met a couple of pilots who came to work for Metro Airlines and were former Great Western pilots. After talking with them I found out that they had both been there after I left. The significance of this is that I was sure those airplanes were on their last legs when I left. How anyone could have flown those things two and even three years more impressed me. I was impressed because, one, those airplanes had lasted that long with that terrible maintenance and, two, those guys had been courageous enough—nay, *crazy* enough—to go out and fly those derelicts.

Chris Cofield is one of these pilots. He related this story to me some time back when we were talking about 202 GW. She was his favorite too, as well as his regular plane.

One of his regular routes was flying into Corpus Christi. In the summertime, coastal areas can be the toughest flying going. Thunderstorms can be almost daily occurrences because of the adequate source of moisture. Great Western was never known to have radar in their Beeches, which made the task of picking a soft spot through which to penetrate the line of storms more than difficult. At best, a Great Western pilot could get a vector from ATC, then ride out whatever came down the chute.

Another thing that Chris was used to doing was striking out on a direction of his own. For some reason, ATC usually could care less what happened to that lowly Great Western crew out there. Therefore, it became customary for the Great Western crews to do most of the choosing on their own.

It was four o'clock in the afternoon, the heat of the day. The sun and the unstable, moist atmosphere combined to make a great wall around the Corpus area. The clouds were a glaring white from the sunny side, masking the feverish intensity of commotion down in their gullett. If Chris and his copilot were to finish their route today, those storms had to be penetrated.

They cruised up and down the line looking for a break in the activity. Center wasn't being much help—as usual. They could circle around all of it and go about 50 miles offshore and come in from the back side. The idea of flying 202 over 50 miles of water seemed like a sure way to the swamps of Hell. A storm penetration might be easier—at least they wouldn't have to swim if 202 gave out.

If you have never done it—flown into thunderstorms, that is—you can't imagine the anxiety that builds up. The nervous stomach and growls from the lower tract all work in concert to make the pilot very uncomfortable. It's nature's way of saying,

"Don't do this, Charlie." Yet when one is working for a freight company the choice is usually "get the freight there or lose your job." That can be an exceptionally strong incentive. And if you think they wouldn't fire a pilot for that, then you have never flown freight or talked to a freight pilot.

That was the situation for Chris that afternoon. His problem was to find a way through and the devil be damned. After what seemed like hours of marching up and down the line, it became evident that the only way to Corpus was through the mess. Chris instructed his co-jock to strap in tight and in his soft-spoken Texas drawl said, "Well, let's go see what it's like." 202 GW had seen this all before, countless times. The logbook said she had. She was a freighter, wasn't she?

It didn't take long before Chris found out that going through wasn't such a great idea, regardless of his job status. It was the worst turbulence he had ever seen—or might *ever* see. The plane was uncontrollable. His flight kit was banging alternately on the celing and the floor. What order there might have been in the cargo bay was long since gone. The yoke was flailing wildly back and forth almost ripping itself out of the floor.

Chris slowed 202 down as much as he dared to minimize the turbulence. It was still pounding them to death. He wrapped his arms around the yoke and pulled it to his chest in an effort to minimize the infernal flailing. Meanwhile, the co-pilot was having one heck of a time just trying to stay in his seat. As tight as his belt was, he had slipped down in the seat to where he was laying flat on his back. Chris later laughed at how funny it looked to see his legs flying this way and that as he was pinned down to the seat. But most spectacular of all was the way 202 GW was riding through this all.

Back on the ground, the co-pilot was swearing that he'd never let Chris do that to him again. It seems that from his inclined position, as his head beat roughly against the window sill, he had seen 202's wings flapping two or three feet up and down during the ordeal. He was white as a ghost—thought they were goners.

Inspection of 202 GW after that flight showed nothing obvious had been overstressed. Her wings looked as solid as ever. Her Pinnochio nose proudly pitched skyward and her big black Minnie Mouse shoes were ready to go walking again. That darned airplane went through all that and was ready to take on a new day.

But what could a pilot expect out of that favored old girl? She was a freighter, wasn't she?

# The Boom Operator

Military operations or life in the Air Force has its peculiarities. For one thing, the military is the only place one might participate in inflight refueling of aircraft. The crews are usually good at what they do, but they weren't born that way. Learning to refuel in the air takes practice. Whenever a refueling crew lacks experience, the procedure can be rough and exciting.

Refueling is done with KC-135 tankers. These are a version of the Boeing 707. Since a KC-135 tanker fueled and ready to go can exceed 300,000 pounds, it has a great inertia in the air. In other words, it takes another large plane to move it around in the air during the refueling exercise.

As I was saying, an inexperienced crew can cause a little bit of trouble during refueling, especially when that crew occupies the trailing ship or the plane that is being refueled. The tanker has the easier job of flying, as all that crew needs to do is to keep their plane flying straight and level. The trailing ship must maneuver behind the tanker into a position from which it can couple onto the fueling boom. This takes a sure hand and a fair amount of experience to make the job go smoothly.

There is one person, however, in the tanker whose job is not that easy. His job can be extremely difficult and frightening if the trailing ship tends to be unsteady due to turbulence or lack of crew skill. That person is, of course, the boom operator. It is his job to wield the boom around at the rear of the tanker and stab the trailing ship at its refueling port. The margins for error are small for every participant in the exercise. It is a coordinated team effort and everyone must take his job very seriously. And most of the time everyone does.

On one particular day the refueling was not to go as smoothly as it could have. The job was to refuel a SAC bomber, a B-52. A B-52 is a mighty large airplane and when in the hands of an inexperienced crew, problems can develop. As the rendevous point was approached, the boom operator went to his position at the rear of the tanker and waited for the B-52 to show up in the window.

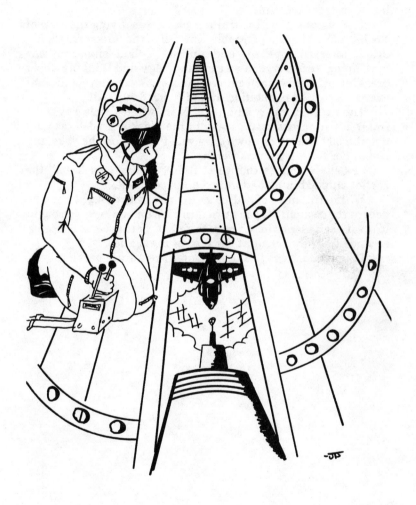

It didn't take long for the boom operator to realize that he was working with a new guy. The B-52 was up and down and even circled the boom. Only the experience of the boom operator allowed the B-52 to be "stabbed" at all that morning. Even after hooking up, the crew of the B-52 continued to fight the situation. The trailing ship thrashed around in the air behind the tanker like a snagged salmon.

The instability of the trailing plane was giving the crew of the KC-135 a handful of trouble. The tail of the tanker was being lifted, swerved, pushed, and pulled. A bad situation was developing and everyone was getting edgy and thinking about breaking off. Under such circumstances it is very important that everyone stay at his station and play heads-up ball.

The captain was grumbling: "Man, where'd this guy come from? I can barely keep us within the block altitude" (usually about 5,000 feet up or down). He was tugging on the yoke and riding her for all she was worth.

"I believe this is the worst flying I have ever seen," the copilot chipped in as he tightened his seat belt.

Within the midst of it all came a comforting thought from the door of the cockpit: "If you guys think it's bad up here, you ought to see it back there where I have to sit." It was the boom operator, escaped from the terror at the rear of the plane.

Like I said, guys in the Air Force are a little peculiar.

# Hide and Seek

Flying for a living can mean that most days are pretty ho-hum. Everyone has heard the old adage "hours of boredom punctuated by moments of stark terror." That pretty much says it for those who fly for their supper. Because this is so true, crews inevitably think up some of the darnedest things to liven up a day.

We've already talked about the boom operator in the tanker service. Because of his relative isolation from the remainder of the crew he was the butt of lots of jokes.

As one tanker finished up a refueling job one afternoon, the captain got an idea. George, the boom operator, was still in the aft of the aircraft.

As if a light had just gone on in his head, Captain Michaels looked around at his crew with a sly grin. "Let's hide down in the 'hell hole' from old George. When he gets back up here the flight deck will be deserted."

"Yeah, ol' George is so superstitious he'll think the 'Ghost of Flight 401' got us," the first officer seconded the idea.

So they set the autopilot going the direction they wanted, lifted the trap door to the "hell hole," and disappeared. A few short minutes later ol' George came forward.

At first he was really spooked. There wasn't another trace of a human on board. He began to talk to himself: "All right, George, there's got to be a completely reasonable explanation here." About that time he thought he felt a thump beneath the cockpit floor.

"Ah, they're down in the 'hell hole' are they? I'll get those suckers for this." George was the one with the devilish grin now. He slid gingerly into the captain's seat, thinking to himself, "No wonder that guy falls asleep at the wheel all the time. This seat's too soft. Now, where's that autopilot?" Grabbing the yoke he found the disengage switch quite by accident. The autopilot lights went out and George, the boom operator, was in full control of that big 250,000-pound bird.

31

He clutched the yoke in both hands like he was about to take his first roller coaster ride. Pushing and pulling on that yoke as if he had hold of a bull, the plane began railing like a beast.

Needless to say, Captain Michaels came shooting out of the trap door to the "hell hole" like a Polaris missile. The look on the captain's face thrilled George to no end. He'd finally gotten one up on the crew.

"For cryin' out loud, George, I thought the autopilot had gone berserk," the captain spouted between gasps for breath.

"Well, when I first came up here, I thought the Ghost of Flight 401 took you guys," George explained.

# In a Green Fog

It's lonely out there, over Hell's Canyon at night. I don't know if it's the terrain, the earth's magnetism, or the fact that it is so far from anywhere. One thing is for sure: They got the name right.

Hell's Canyon is the great enclosure that engulfs the formidable Snake River. It runs between Idaho and Oregon in a remote region that is known for its lack of roads and the overwhelming Seven Devils range. From the air, on a clear day, the spectacle induces a feeling of awe.

At night, on the other hand, the sky is almost always cloudy, hiding the great chasm. In the back of one's mind lurks the realization that not too far below, the terrain is rising and falling thousands of feet at a crack as the plane races ahead. It is no place to be forced into a landing, for at night, it would be hopeless. It tends to reinforce one's character. One unfortunate soul ran out of gas there in the dead of winter. They finally got his body out four months later.

Well, this story isn't about the canyon, but it sets the stage for the strangest occurence in my flying career. More than once, incidents over Hell's Canyon have filled my heart with terror. If I ever had to fly over that place again at night, it would be too soon.

Great Western Airlines had a mail contract to fly the mail between Spokane, Lewiston, and Boise, Idaho. They also had a pilot to fly that route in a dirty old weather-beaten Aztec with a bad engine. That idiot was *me*. Mountains, ice, thunderstorms, and enough fuel were the normal considerations. Those were the things I considered to be tangible. The intangible considerations were Hell's Canyon and the Salmon River (Of No Return) canyon. It seemed like something weird was always happening out there between Boise and Lewiston.

It was early June 1977 and thunderstorms had come to the northern Rockies. Most of them had dissipated by my 12:30 A.M. departure time out of Boise. As the Aztec began its labored climb northbound, I noticed a distant flash on the horizon at my two

33

o'clock position. It was nothing to be alarmed about since it didn't appear to be on my route of flight. I filed it away for future reference and forgot about the flash.

After leaving 6,000 feet I could clear the first mountainous obstacles near the entrance of the Salmon River canyon. The controller cleared me on course as I continued to climb to 12,000 feet. Somewhere about 10,000 feet I went into the soup. It was solid IFR and was a very normal thing to have happen. Tuning in KOB, an Albuquerque radio station, I settled in for the hour and a half flight back to Lewiston.

About 40 minutes had passed and Hell's Canyon was getting close. The clouds remained, encapsulating the plane in a milky gray fog. That's when my senses became challenged by the extraordinary. A dim flash caught my attention and drew me away from the instrument panel. It wasn't exactly a flash. It was more like a flicker—a *green* flicker. The obvious thing to do was check my right wingtip to see if my green navigation light was flickering. It wasn't; steady as could be.

By the time I'd done the checking, the green flicker had grown into a steady glow. The light in the clouds was growing quickly to an almost daylight quality. The once-gray capsule around the plane was now an intense lime green. In every direction the sight was the same—green fog! And then it dimmed, flickered as if it were a candle being extinguished by the wind, and went out.

"Center, this Great Western 612. Are you painting any thunderstorms in this area?" I was fishing for an answer, *any* kind of answer.

"Well, uh, no; there's some about 70 miles east of you," he sleepily drawled. That's the one's I had seen after takeoff.

"Well, you're not gonna believe this. The clouds just lit up a bright lime green all around the plane. I mean it lasted from four to seven seconds as near as I can figure." I winced at how absurd that sounded in the middle of the night.

"Uh, yeah, roger 612," the controller obviously thought I was drunk, hallucinating or had been flying the mail for too long. I didn't blame him. It's hard to imagine anything like what I witnessed really happening.

Well, in the years since that night I've done some hypothesizing. Meteorites will burn green if they contain copper—just the color of green I saw that night. So maybe a meteorite came down through the clouds near me. I watched the news and newspapers for several days in hopes of seeing a report to that effect. No such luck.

Another possibility could be that a UFO came up behind me and flashed his lights to pass. I doubt it.

So what the heck was it? Any ideas? Well, I have one more: It could be the terrain, the Earth's magnetism—or the fact that it is *so* far from anywhere.

# The Payback

One of an airline pilot's major daily considerations is staying on schedule. There's a great number of things that can disrupt the best intentions. For example, ticket agents may board flights late, fuel trucks don't show up or break down, or controllers issue circuitous clearances. This story addresses the latter. It is another pilot-controller story.

At the outset I should say that the Air Traffic Control system works fairly well most of the time. Controllers make an effort to keep traffic flowing smoothly to and from the airport. On occasion, however, what the controller thinks is a good deal and what the flight crew considers a good deal just don't jive. That sets the stage for a conflict.

There are two important facets to this story that deserve some explanation in order for you to fully enjoy it. First, the airplane concerned here is a deHavilland Twin Otter. Now, the Twin Otter was designed as a short takeoff and landing (STOL) aircraft. Its top speed in a descent is either 156 knots or 171 knots, depending on the particular model. But what is impressive is its *low* speed. It's only 60 knots with full flaps extended. This speed allows the airplane to be highly adaptable to bush-type flying. The funny thing is that at Metro Airlines, with the exception of two airports, there is no need for that slow-speed handling. The upshot is that the controllers at the larger airports (namely Dallas-Fort Worth) have seen very little of the STOL capabilities of the plane. It can prove to be an almost unbelievable sight, as we shall see later.

The second important factor to this tale is the personality of one Captain Scott Stanton. Scott was a New Yorker, a dyed-in-the-wool Yankee. That may raise the dander of any New Yorkers reading this book, but it isn't meant to be a statement of any prejudice. The truth is that whenever a New Yorker is thrust into a laid-back Texas environment, the effect is like two immiscible fluids.

Scott might not have been Irish, but he looked and played the part. He is over six feet tall with bristly red hair. Although he was liked by most everyone at the airline (he now flies for Piedmont), we all had a feeling he was on the verge of eruption most of the time. His pungent New York accent and continual sarcasm at the inane Texan way of doing things tended to indicate a close proximity to the boiling point. Most of the things Scott would let go with struck me as funny because he was usually right. It was just that things that seemed insignificant to others were a big deal to him.

As we mentioned in an earlier story in this book, the runway assignments at the DFW airport leave a lot to be desired. Remember the Metro-Rio race? Well, it is the east side (17L/35R) that is the coveted runway due to its proximity to the terminal. Landing on the west side involves a 10 minute taxi under the best traffic conditions. On the other hand, landing on 17L usually only involves turning off the runway and taxiing to the terminal—a time of about two minutes at most.

Well, everyone going into DFW gets their share of landing on the "wrong side." Braniff hated the east side because their terminal was on the west. American and Delta were like us; they wanted the east runway. Every company tries to avoid getting the "wrong" runway by making offers such as extending their downwind, following traffic in sight, or slowing down. But not Scott. He was going to force it if he could.

Scott must have gotten what he thought was more than his share of the wrong runway. To a commuter pilot who flies into to DFW several times a day, it can and does get irritating. It all led to Scott getting fed up.

"Metro 1022 contact approach on 132.1." The initial approach controller handed Scott's flight off to the final sequence controller.

"Metro 1022," they crackled back and changed frequency.

"Approach, Metro 1022 with you." Terry Martin, the first officer, did his job matter-of-factly.

"Metro 1022, do you have the airport in sight?" the controller asked.

"Affirmative."

"You're number one for the right, make short approach." The instructions had been given; an ax had fallen just where it shouldn't have.

Back in the cockpit, Scott was fuming. He yanked the power off and set the Otter to lumbering through the air. With flaps fully extended, the airspeed sank to a mere 60 knots. It didn't take long for the controller to notice something was going on. You can almost picture him tapping his radar screen to see if 1022's dot or blip was stuck.

"Metro 1022, keep your speed up," came the imperative call from the controller.

"Uh sir, Metro 1022 is at final approach speed," Scott challenged.

"Well, can you give me any more?" The controller was trying to avoid an altercation if possible.

Scott came back with: "Well, maybe."

"Well then, what can you give me?" the controller querried.

Scott was fed up to his eyeballs with this sort of service. His answer was typically Stantonish: "I can give you 160 knots to the left or 60 knots to the right!"

# A Proper Lady

It's hard to believe these days that airlines once flew the Convairs like they do Boeings now. Braniff, American, Frontier, Texas International (Trans Texas Airways)—all had them. Frankly, much of the romance of those days was built around the old "round tail" airplanes like the Convairs and DC-3s. Most of that atmosphere is gone, what with airlines floundering to make ends meet and offering no-frills flights. That's probably what makes these old stories so appealing.

It has been said so many times before that life was simpler back then. People were more naive. The simplest thing could conjure up feelings of terror when it wasn't understood. Such was the case in this hangar tale that a veteran American Airlines stewardess (from the days before they were called flight attendants) related to me.

The flight was a Convair 580 from Dallas to Oklahoma City. It was loaded with Texans and Okies to the gills. It just figures that the crew, based in Dallas, was overrun with Texans. The first officer was one of those East Texas lads who spoke with a twang that could be heard clear back to Georgia. His expressions and command of the vernacular were as backwoods as cornpone and sweet-potato pie.

As the boarding began, a particular young lady stood out from the rest—it was her air of conceit, with her nose five feet in the air. She was complaining about the lack of a first class compartment; just downright snotty.

Well, as most flights go, this one was as unspiritual as they come. After arrival at the gate and the parking brake had been locked the crew called for the toilet to be serviced. Not all the passengers deplaned at Oklahoma City. Some of them were continuing on to Tulsa for the next stop. As the propellers stopped swinging, the ground crew began unloading and loading baggage.

It was then that this Dallas socialite got up and went to the john. On the trip to OKC her mein hadn't changed. First the coffee was too hot and then it was too bitter; it was just one thing

after another. In short, she had been the south end of a northbound mule.

As the door to the john was closing inside the plane, the ground crew was hooking up the toilet servicing machine outside the plane. Now, the way service is accomplished is that the entire contents of the chemical toilet are drained. Then this bright blue chemical is pumped in under pressure through the flush ports inside the toilet bowl.

When the latter part of this operation began there came a horrendous scream from the toilet. The door to the john was flung open and this very proper Dallas lady limped into the companionway with her girdle down around her knees, flailing, screaming, and dripping in blue toilet chemicals. She was next to incoherent. It was all much to the delight of the other passengers.

It was at this moment the copilot came through the door of the cockpit and into the companionway. He took a look at this woman and in his perfect east Texan drawl spoke: "Ma'am I believe you fergot to pull your drawers up. And I believe that's just a tad on the bawdy side for Okie City."

# Who Said That?

A great many things went on during the first few days of the controllers' strike of 1981. The air traffic system was balled up from coast to coast. Although there were regular reports from various airline pilots that the system was working better than ever, that was not always the case. There were many delays that most of us were not used to seeing and being number 13 or 14 for takeoff can test the patience of the best of crews.

During one enormous backlash, tempers were just about to flare. To be fair, the backlash was not due to the taxed air traffic control system, but to bad weather along many of the routes. Even so, the radio kept crackling with requests like, "How long for American 454?"

The controllers would retaliate with: "American 454, I have no idea. I'll call you when I am notified by flow control."

Every airline had a request and usually the answer was the same: The tower controllers just were not able to give the airlines the information they needed to pass on to their passengers and companies.

Finally, one pilot from an unidentified airplane near the end of the runway broke in over the frequency and said, in a slow Texas drawl, "Boy, this really sucks!"

There was no mistake that the tower controller had heard the comment. He ripped back on the frequency with, "All right, who said that?"

And the answer came:

"Braniff."

"American."

"Delta."

"Ozark."

The controller was beat and knew it. He decided to be a good sport about the whole thing: "Now gentlemen," (there was a little pause) *"that's* brotherhood."

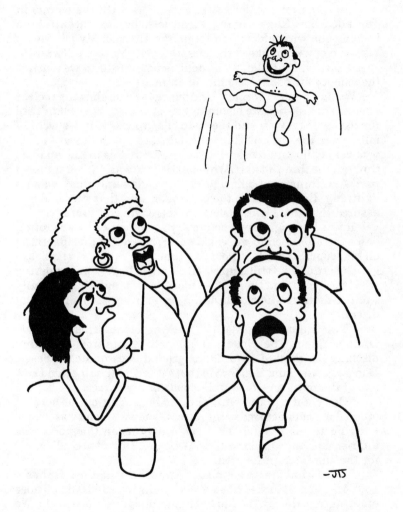

then it started throwing the Twin Otter around like a ping-pong ball in the surf. Passengers in the back were screaming. I was to find out why, later.

The amazing thing about all this turbulence was that we were in the clear—no clouds, no rain, just invisible shearing winds that were visibly shaking everyone up.

This was my copilot's first experience with the storms in Tornado Alley. He was flying. I instructed him to concentrate on keeping the wings level and forget the altitude. My job was to vary the power and keep the airspeed near $V_a$ or maneuvering speed. Everything went as normal as possible until we reached the smooth air behind the line of storms.

We had made it through and our radar was showing it clear ahead. That's when we began to get concerned. We couldn't see the lights of Lawton and the controller was saying we were 17 miles from the airport. The controller, an acquaintance of mine, was very calm and reassuring as he vectored us to line up to go through the thinnest part. What puzzled me was, *"What* thinnest part?" Nothing was painting on our radar and there was no lightning. Ben Martinez, the controller, said that we could rest assured that there was something there. We continued.

It was like countdown before a space shot. Ben was counting down the miles before we would enter the area of precip returns on his scope. Six miles to go: I fine-tuned our radar. Five miles to go: The radar was still empty. Three miles to go: I'm wondering what the heck is out there. Even more, I am wondering if I really want to do this. The clouds still haven't lit up with a lightning discharge.

"Two more miles, Metro." Nothing on the radar, but *oh,* what a flash! The clouds lit up with a multiple lightning discharge. I glanced towards the ground to estimate the bases. Don't ask why I did that, but in that second of illumination I saw one of the most awesome wall clouds of my career.

"One-eighty to the left John, we're getting out of here," I ordered my copilot to make the retreat. The wall cloud was nearly hanging to the ground. That could only mean the storm was angrier than any airplane alive. We weren't about to challenge it for the dominion of Lawton.

"Now, what are we gonna do?" my cohort inquired. He had a good question. It looked like we were going back to Dallas. Those other storms, though, had to be circumnavigated once again. We weren't relishing that task. The strange thing was that once we were headed back the way we came, the radar painted the first line of storms as well as it had the first time. To this day I am puzzled why the second line never showed up.

On the way into Dallas we became painfully aware that our

unusual amount of deviation had eaten away our reserve fuel. Center wanted to route us the regular roundabout way to Dallas. We insisted on direct. He asked us if we were declaring an emergency. My reply was that we were not unless he would not give us direct. Then we would have an emergency and he'd have to route us direct anyhow. He weighed the possibilities and gave us direct to DFW.

Arriving at DFW we had about 18 minutes of fuel left. Why didn't we go somewhere closer? The storms covered all options and were moving towards Dallas with incredible speed. The passengers were glad to be on solid ground. So was the crew.

About 1:00 A.M. that next morning, the storms that were a hundred miles away in Lawton had moved through Dallas. We boarded the passengers who were left to fly to Lawton. We only lost three or four, which is not many considering the turbulence and long wait for the storms to pass through Dallas.

The second flight to Lawton was smooth and starry. But the most entertaining part of the night, at least to me, occurred when we arrived at Lawton. After completing the shutdown checklist, I walked through the terminal on the way to our crew room. I could scarely believe what I overheard. Here was this lady talking to someone who'd met her at the terminal about a little boy about eight years old who had been on our first flight around the storms. It sounded something like this:

"My God, Charlie, it was *so* rough! This little boy fell to the ceiling while we were upside down." She was sure that it was true. She really believed we were upside down.

"Upside down? You mean it got so rough that the plane turned upside down?" Her friend was doubting the story. I sped up my pace to hurry by them. I didn't want to become a part of that conversation.

We were not upside down, of course. What did happen was that a downdraft caused negative Gs in the airplane and the boy floated—albeit rather quickly—to the ceiling. He did not have his seat belt buckled.

Sure, I could have stopped and explained, but I figured someone who believed we were upside down would never understand the physics of what really did happen.

# The Old Pawnee

David Frazier, did a fine job in his book *The ABC's of Safe Flying*. (TAB #2290). In the introduction, he relates a story about two mechanics at an FBO who are rebuilding the engine on an old Pawnee. It's such a good story I thought I would include it here.

It was a small operation in Texas, a place where the good ol' boys liked to hang out. They'd come to the hangar when the summer heat would get too much for sitting in the cockpits of their singles. They'd hunker down next to the toolbench and regale each other and the mechanics trying to make a living with war stories.

Out behind the repair shop sat an old Pawnee. It hadn't flown in so long the birds and mud daubers had made it their home. Months of Texas sun had baked the paint into oblivion. The Pawnee looked bedraggled and unquestionably unairworthy.

The abject appearance of the Pawnee led to a running controversy of several days. This controversy was between a mature, experienced, and confident mechanic and a young yet equally confident—tenderfoot mechanic. The battle was over whether the old Pawnee would ever run again. The old hand said he'd have it ready in a few days while the tenderfoot just slapped his legs and laughed. The young mechanic thought that the best thing to do would be jack up the canopy, roll a new airplane under it, then replace the canopy. It became a great spectator sport for all the good ol' boys to go out to the hangar and start an argument between the two.

Finally, a slack period hit and the mechanics had time to devote to the old Pawnee. They wheeled the plane in the hangar, suddenly the hottest betting parlor east of Las Vegas. The first thing to go was the chemical tank. Slowly, all the unnecessary items were peeled from the old Indian, to be cleaned and repaired. Next, they poured a solvent into the cylinders and pulled the prop through for a time.

All the time this was going on, the tenderfoot was working his jaw and laughing at the entire idea. Nevertheless, the old mechanic quietly maintained his confidence throughout and kept the labor on the Pawnee organized. However, as they later found out some important items had been overlooked in the reassembly of the Pawnee.

At last the great moment was at hand. The hangar was full of onlookers, bystanders, gawkers, and plain old knee-slappers. They backed the rebuilt duster from the hangar and turned it 90 degrees from the door so the prop blast would be directed away from the shop. A few last insults were traded and the old mechanic started for the cockpit. The youngster said he wasn't going to climb up in the cockpit and waste his energy. He was sure nothing was going to happen. And with that he sauntered over to the wingtip nearest the door and leaned against the plane.

When the old mechanic hollered to "Clear the prop," the believers backed away and the doubters guffawed. It wasn't long before it was apparent to everyone present that the entire area ought to be evacuated. No more than two blades chomped the wind before the engine was agonizing at top of its manifolds. In their haste to complete the job on the duster, the throttle linkage had been assembled backwards. The throttle appearing to be at idle was, in fact, at full power.

In a matter of seconds, huge grey-black clouds of smoke poured from the engine into the vacant compartment that had held the chemical tank and into the cockpit. As the smoke oozed from the doors of the cockpit it was dispersed by the propeller's stiff slipstream. The aircraft began to roll. The younger mechanic grabbed the left wing and held on. This little action was enough to cause the Pawnee to veer away from a new Aero Commander parked ahead and towards the metal shop building. Before chewing into the shop the duster managed to shear off an exposed water pipe. Water began gushing into the air like Yellowstone's finest.

The action from the cockpit was hilarious. The only noticeable reactions during the entire incident were the flailing arms of the old mechanic attempting to extricate himself from the smoke and runaway airplane.

Finally, the aircraft completed its turn and began chomping big chunks out of the metal building. It ate its way down to the wing root and became suddenly quiet.

The water was still cascading into the air as the smoke began to clear. The mechanic crawled down from the ruined duster, now half-buried into the side of the building. Without saying a word, he walked quickly around the rear of the plane and got right in the tenderfoot's face. As the younger one stared wide-eyed into the old hand's grimace, he could scarcely believe what he heard. The old mechanic, seemingly unaffected by the last few seconds of drama, spat out these words in the tenderfoot's face:

"See, I *told* ya it would start!"

# Round and Round She Goes

The table was spread from end to end with a plastic gingham table cloth. On top was a pot luck assortment of extraordinarily good-looking picnic foods punctuated by the pungent aroma of hickory smoked barbeque. Appetites were soaring. Beyond the end of the table stood the thirst-quenchers—two large, old-fashioned wooden barrels packed to the top with ice and beer. All in all, a midsummer's dream.

The gala at hand was the effort of a central Oklahoma flying club, a celebration of summer. Held next to a hangar at the uncontrolled field, the conversations had to turn to flying. The hum of planes making the pattern and occasional taste of 80 octane on the wind was giving at least one of the partygoers the itch to fly.

Now, I really don't know who the principal in this story was. However, a friend of mine told me this tale and he was along for the ride that day, We'll call the instigator Charles, and my friend, Monte.

After an hour or so, big dents had been made in the potato salad and barbeque. Even larger dents had been made in the beer. Charles had had his share and his bravado was growing. "We need some entertainment to liven this party up. How about having our own airshow?"

"Who's gonna fly?" someone asked from the back of the group.

"Well, I will," said Charles.

"Don't you think you've had too many beers to fly?" another voice asked.

"Ah, beer don't effect you like that: I can fly just fine!" Charles was indignant that someone thought he couldn't hold his liquor or fly well.

It was then that Monte, who hadn't had much to drink, spoke up and said he'd go with him just for safety. So off the two went, disappearing into a shadowy hangar. They got a little Cessna 150 out and cranked her up. Minutes later they were airborne.

Both pilots were flight instructors and should have known better than to fly under the influence of alcohol. If they had only realized they were tipsy, they probably wouldn't have dared to go.

From behind the hangar the muted sound of the airborne One-Fifty grew louder. It zoomed overhead, barely clearing the hangar tops. Another low pass down the runway and Charles pulled the little plane straight up to near a stall. He pitched it over in a perfect split-S, and then began a climb.

The Cessna 150 struggled to five or six thousand feet. Down below, the picnickers were anxiety-ridden. No one had tried to stop them, so now they all held their breaths to see what would transpire. The engine suddenly became silent. From the ground it appeared the nose pitched up slightly, then plunged vertically as the wings began to rotate. They were spinning.

Now, the purpose of this story is not to debate whether or not Cessna 150s react adversely after three turns in a spin. However, you ought to be aware that such a controversy exists. Reports have been made that after three turns in a spin, A C-150 is so deeply stalled that it is difficult to recover—damn near impossible is what I've heard.

Well, Charles and Monte were tightening the spin with each progressive turn. After three turns Charles began the normal recovery procedure. Remember, his actions were probably too slow after his imbibing on the ground.

Altitude soon became a precious commodity. Four turns, five turns, finally the beginning of the sixth—the One-Fifty disappeared behind the trees. A sick feeling swept over the onlookers. Suddenly the little two-seater shot up over the hill, moving like lightning. They never had to add power to make the landing. In fact, the landing was too long due to excessive airspeed. The little plane was wrestled to the runway, taxied in, and shut down. The partygoers ran over to the plane, cheering, impressed with the drama of what they thought to be a contrived stunt.

Charles could barely pour himself out of the cockpit. Both pilots were drenched in cold sweat. White-faced, white-knuckled, and weak-kneed, Charles supported himself with various parts of the plane.

"Man, that was fantastic, Charles," was the general comment from those in attendance.

"Hey, Charles, where are you going?" someone asked.

"Home, to sober up, and then to church to thank God. That's where I'm going." With that, Charles disappeared toward the parking lot.

# God's own Hand

"Gray hair," he said, "that's what it'll give you." I was talking with Richard, a former copilot of mine, now turned captain. We were discussing the early days of our careers when we were flight instructing. "By God, if you weren't scared half to death by the situation a greenhorn student had got you into, then you were worried about paying the rent." There was a short pause and he looked me right in the eye and said, "Hell, some things never change."

I had to agree with him. The equipment is a lot bigger now, maybe better, but the money doesn't go any further. "But instructing," I reflected for a moment, "just seemed to be a little more exciting. It seemed to stimulate my interest—well, love—for aviation a great deal more than these airborne Greyhounds.

"Yeah," he said in a strong Texan dialect (he used to be a rodeo cowboy), "but it wasn't what a student did to me that came closest to sending me to the barn for good. It was what I did to us." Richard was off and running.

"We were out in the practice area; had been doing airwork, stalls, and that sort of stuff. This student was getting fairly close to solo and I thought it was time to teach him forced landing precautions and techniques." He paused to take a breath and collect his thoughts. "Well, I was really feeling like Captain America that day. I realize I could have just retarded the throttle and simulated the whole thing, but I thought it would make more of an impression to shut it down altogether. I reached over and pulled out the mixture control."

"When that engine went silent I swallowed hard. It was a little spooky, but I ignored it; acted like I did this all the time." I raised my eyebrow and let him proceed. I couldn't wait to hear if he got started or walked home that day.

We ran through the flow pattern type checklist that is good to use when there isn't time to read one. Of course, we overlooked the mixture purposely to carry the simulation to the limit. At first—I guess he was like most students—he couldn't decide on a landing spot. We discussed the pros and cons of a field versus a road and finally settled on a field. It was a real nice wheatfield better than three-quarters of a mile long. There was a fence and trees at both ends.

"We set up a normal landing pattern as we lost altitude to land. I intended to cross the trees at the approach end of the wheatfield and restart the engine at that point, then have the student execute a go-around. As we crossed the trees, I pushed the mixture in. The prop had stopped windmilling long ago, so I engaged the starter. A few blades went by and nothing happened. I guess it had gotten cold.

"So now there were two factors demanding my attention. Things were piling up. I had to keep trying the restart, but ensure that if we landed it would be before we got to the fence at the other end."

All during his storytelling, Richard had been pushing and pulling on imaginary controls and using all sorts of explanatory gestures. Then he stopped—and started twisting on his moustache. He must have been back in that little trainer, fighting the battle of skill, luck, and destiny. And me? I was dying to know how this war story was going to end.

"My instructions," Richard finally continued, "to the student were simple: 'Get ready to make a normal flare and landing. I'll keep cranking.' We were Gosh-awful low now and we could hear the wheat whipping the tires. Grasshoppers and bugs were smashing on the windshield and that stupid engine just kept going *ar-ar-ar-ar*. I looked up for a second and could tell that if we landed, we wouldn't stop before the fence."

"Then, as if God's own hand had come down and warmed the little engine, she caught. I yelled 'I got it,' and fed the power in smoothly. We cleared the fence and luckily shot through about a 50-foot gap between two trees.

"Back on the ground at the airport I told the student to just hang onto his logbook and I'd sign it the next time. With that I started for the parking lot. The student was a little perplexed and yelled to me and asked where I was going."

"Home," I yelled back. He wanted to know why.

"'To change my underwear, that's why!'"

Back in the real world now, I looked at Richard. "Gray hair, eh? That doesn't seem like the only thing instructing gave you!"

# Big John

In the maturing of any company, many things happen over the months and years that result in the institution of policies. For example, single-engine practice will not be performed during flying the route, even if the flight is empty. Now, that little policy came from an incident at our airline about the second year of operation. It's funny now to think that is not just common sense. But back when this story happened, it was common for the captains to give the first officers a little on-the-job-training when flights were empty. Probably the two things that seem most odd now is that we don't practice single-engine procedures at all except check rides, and it has been a long time since the flights were empty.

As has been mentioned before in this book, the staple airplane for Metro Airlines has been the Twin Otter. Its remarkable flight characteristics make this hangar tale understandable and believable. To those who have never flown a multi-engine aircraft, bear in mind that asymmetrical power will cause an airplane to turn. Also, a propeller coming out of feather will produce one whale of a power surge.

Big John was what they called him: he was about the biggest man you could stuff in a Twin Otter cockpit. He wasn't a man of many words—the quiet type. Nonetheless, most of the copilots liked to fly with him because he was experienced and tended to take the fatherly approach to giving advice and imparting knowledge. His reputation as an impeccable pilot and one generally unruffled in tight situations was justified. But this time his unruffled manner was what got him in trouble.

The airport was Houston Hobby. In the control tower, an alert controller was watching the Twin Otter through binoculars. As the plane drew nearer, what the controller had at first suspected became apparent. One propeller was feathered, but the engine was still turning it at an idle speed.

"Metro, any problems?" The controller was referring to the feathered prop. However, the crew was just practicing a single-engine approach. The flight was empty, a fact unknown to the controller.

"Nope," is all Big John came back with.

"Well, cleared to land." In the Twin Otter, the approach was going normally. Of course, the controller was still worried about a scheduled flight with only one engine running correctly.

The landing procedure for an Otter is for the props to be pushed forward on touchdown. It's a habit, pure and simple. In a single-engine situation, the prop on the operating engine is already pushed forward. The feathered prop would need to be pushed forward in order to taxi.

As the main wheels touched the runway, Big John, sitting in the right seat, pushed the feathered prop forward. The copilot was relatively inexperienced and was the only one who could control the nosewheel steering.

As we mentioned at the outset, a prop that is brought out of feather will cause a forward power surge. Since only one prop was feathered, the power surge was asymmetrical. That was enough. As the prop came out of feather it yawed the Otter to the left. The copilot lost control and the plane bounded crazily across the infield between runways and taxiway.

The normal reaction for Big John would be to reach down with his left hand, grab the nose wheel tiller bar, and get the airplane under control. Sitting in the right seat as he was, his left hand was filled with air. The copilots left hand might as well have been filled with air as his attempts to control the plane were only making the situation worse.

Big John was now reduced to his next choice, reversing the props to stop the plane's forward progress. Why he didn't jump on the brakes we'll never know. He just pulled the power levers back into the reverse range. If you know anything about PT-6 engines, you know that rarely will two engines spool-up in reverse at the same time. It's another case of asymmetrical power, only now in reverse.

The controller watching the Otter veer off the runway was concerned for other traffic nearby. "Metro, are you all right?"

"Yep," was Big John's matter-of-fact answer. That's when the right engine reversed first and the Otter careened back to the right and onto a taxiway. Frustrated by the lack of available control (mainly nosewheel steering), Big John threw the throttles forward and was airborne—on the taxiway!

"Uh, Metro . . . " The controller didn't know quite what to say. "Cleared for takeoff or cleared to land or taxi to the ramp. Just tell me what you are doing!"

"Uh, Tower? We'd like to come back around and land." Big John made an in-depth request for him.

"Well, then, you're cleared to land, runway of your choice," the controller shot back.

As the Twin Otter circled the pattern for another go at it, the policy-making process began in earnest. The tower controller made telephone contact with Metro's Director of Operations: "Sir, I don't know what flight 358 was up to. Let's suffice it to say that they took off from a taxiway. I won't even tell you the rest. I think you should talk to the captain. I mean, he gave us no advisory on his intentions whatsoever."

Indeed, Big John had been quiet as usual. Of course, the speed at which things happened didn't leave much time to elaborate.

Well, this particular story doesn't have a funny ending. It does, however, show how policies come about. In this case, no single-engine practice is allowed other than in training flights or checkrides. Is it any wonder?

# The Van Arsdale's Secret

Back through five decades of foggy nights and bright days and beautiful sunrises, we come to a little boy and his father sliding through a cool New England morning in a biplane. The father deftly steered the old *Waco* through a series of dips and dives, loops and rolls. Then the little boy flashed his father a prearranged signal. He lifted his index finger high in the air where his father in the rear cockpit could see it. Then the old *Waco* slowly rolled upside down, to the delight of the young boy.

The young boy's name was John Van Arsdale. He was never to outgrow his love for aviation. Those cool flights of New England mornings were in his blood forever. Upon graduating from high school John enrolled in a commercial aviation course in college and did very well. In the Army Air Corps he concentrated on meteorology, where he built up a wealth of weather savvy.

Discharge from the Army brought John to the jumping-off point we all reach eventually—what to do with the rest of his life. He decided to keep on flying and founded the Provincetown-Boston Airline. With an unlikely beginning, the airline grew from two J-3 Cubs and a PT-17 to a much larger and successful airline. Today the airline has planes operating in New England and Florida. As a matter of fact, the world's oldest (flying hours) DC-3 breaks a record every day it flies under the PBA banner.

For all these years the Van Arsdales kept the secret, about the little boy in the biplane but it's okay now. John Van Arsdale is well past his flying prime and the secret is out.

For all his aviation expertise and countless hours in the air, John Van Arsdale could never shake his disease—motion sickness. Every flight of his life John flew with the controls in one hand and a sick sack in the other. And remember that little

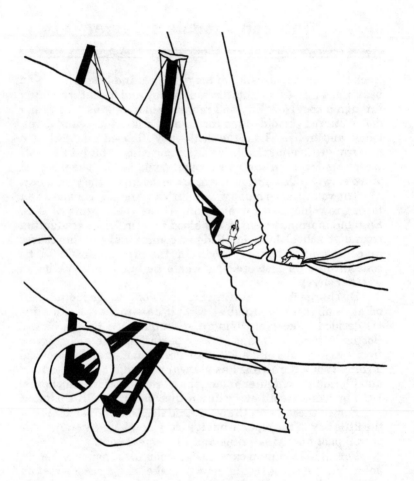

boy in the biplane? His raised finger was a signal for his father to roll the plane upside down so he could throw up—upside down, of course.*

*Adapted and retold from a Paul Harvey "The Rest of the Story."

# Where the Buffalo Roam

The old-timers used to say an east wind blows ill. Of course, they were speaking of the impending gales that usually follow. The remote possibility that they were referring to hot air balloons is doubtful. However, hot air balloons are but drifters on the wind and in this case the east wind blew ill for its pilot.

The setting is north Dallas during the evening rush hour. It had been a beautiful day with clear skies and a light east or southeast wind. Taking advantage of the fair evening, a balloon pilot drifted lazily westward, enjoying the cooling temperatures and the freedom from the traffic jams below. It was not to last.

I don't know what might have been the problem, since I know so very little about ballooning and this story came to me third-hand. The pilot of that large airborne dinosaur, however, either mismanaged his fuel or was the poorest judge of a good landing spot of any pilot alive. One thing for sure, Murphy's Law was operating at full tilt. Everything was going wrong for this guy that could go wrong. One of the corollaries—that one will be in the wrong place at the right time—was also being applied to this poor unfortunate.

The pilot reached up and gave two or three blasts on his burner to gain altitude. His red balloon was hanging on the wind like a big jellyfish caught in a sea current. The immediate problem was to cross the power lines that would surely ensnare this gargantuan. It was a simple enough project on a normal day, but today nothing was working very well. Another long burst on the burner and the basket barely cleared the wires.

With that event now in his recent past, the pilot became confounded by the next. The balloon continued to lose lift, rather quickly now. Silently it slid down into the rush hour traffic, which was about to become mixed with air traffic in an unlikely fashion. The basket came to squat right in the middle of highway 289.

Automobiles came to a halt and began to jam up on being confronted with so huge an object and one obviously commanding the right of way. The pilot's face was a red as the shroud

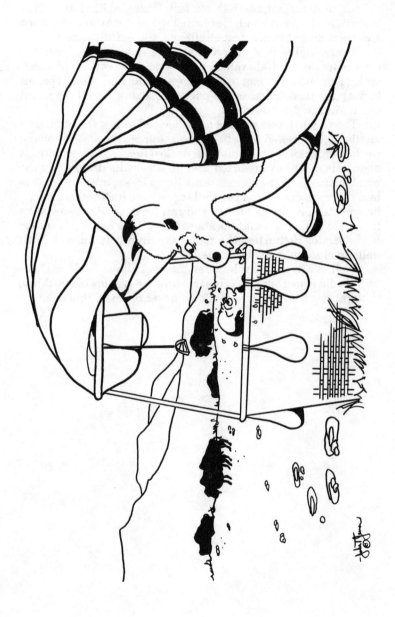

above him. Tugging at the burner cans, the pilot coaxed the balloon to rise a foot, two feet, ten feet. It seemed like hours for it to move in the light wind. He cleared the highway and the fence and went on to his greatest challenge, the buffalo ranch.

That's right, this poor fellow was having a balloonist's nightmare on a buffalo ranch. At this point he ran out of ideas, options, or both. The bag of hot air was going limp, fast. It began to drag the basket across the pasture, looking for all the world like a giant red tumbleweed.

That's when two mature bulls decided to test the intruder's mettle. They lowered their heads and charged the basket and the world's unluckiest balloonist. He ducked inside as they batted it about. He must have realized that he was being dragged by the wind farther from the nearest fence line, sure separation from his beefy tormentors. As the two bulls drew back for another charge, he squirted out of the basket and ran for dear life towards the fence. He ran so fast that his shoes flew off his feet, but he never broke stride. He hurtled the fence like an olympian with both bulls in close pursuit. He made it.

Well, we're not sure how he got his balloon back or if the buffalo did something imaginative to it. We *are* sure of one thing, though: His beer-drinking buddies never believed this one.

# Burden, Kansas

Out there on the Plains lies the town of Burden, Kansas. Late summer, perhaps early fall brings the annual rodeo to town. Now, there aren't too many ways to get to Burden. There are no trains, no airports very close; just the road and one other way—making a path through the tall corn.

Too late to drive to Burden for the rodeo, an alternative had to be found if Richard was going to make it to the competition. He decided to fly. He chose a Cessna mixmaster, a plane owned by several friends. As darkness encroached upon the sky and the ground below, the Skymaster drew close to Burden. Richard could see the lights of the arena near town. He had planned to land at an airport in nearby Winfield, but now could see that he had arrived later than he expected. He descended lower and lower and made some passes close to the arena. Things were in progress and he began to worry about whether he would get down and find transportation to the competition.

Circling as he weighed the choices, Richard twisted the knob on his radio to 122.8 MHz. Back at that time, it was the standard Unicom frequency and it was a lucky twist. A voice came over the radio: "Uh, airplane circling the Burden rodeo arena, uh, you need a place to land?"

Richard wondered who might have seen him. He wondered why they would have a radio on his frequency out here in the middle of nowhere. Was it another plane? He picked the mike up, "Well, yeah, I was going to land at Winfield. Where are you?"

"Well, I've got a little duster strip about a quarter mile west of the arena. You are going to the rodeo aren't ya?" The voice seemed to be offering a helping hand.

"Yeah, I'm entered in the saddle bronc ridin' and need to get there pretty soon. How long's your strip?" Richard spoke with that drawl, Texan to the core.

"Well, its about 2500 feet long. There's some power lines at the north end and the wind is from the south. You're gonna have to cross 'em to land. But, if you want to, I'll park my pickup at the other end with lights on. You can line up with the lights and

land." The voice had a plan all right, but could the airplane get in that little strip over those wires in the twilight?

Richard found the lights of the pickup. Lining the mix-master up with them, he made a pass to find the wires and circled for the "final" approach. He slowed the airplane to hang out all the flaps, but he had a slight case of nerves. The approach was way too high and hot. The airplane shot over the wires and toward the pickup truck. He forced the plane to the turf. It looked like a motorized, high-speed, three-legged milk stool.

It didn't take him long to realize that he was going to need some drastic braking to get stopped before sawing into the front end of the pickup. The brakes locked up and the plane began to fishtail violently, kicking up a cloud of dust. The driver of the pickup truck began to realize that his number might be up. He slammed the truck into reverse and it began to fishtail and kick up its own dust. Obviously, the airplane, with its two buzzing props, had the edge in this contest of chicken.

The Skymaster slid to a stop just in front of the truck, which was still in a full-power retreat to the rear. When it appeared to be safe, the farmer returned. He threw open his door and walked over to the plane as the props ticked to a stop.

"My God, I thought you were going to kill us both! Is your plane all right?" He was obviously concerned.

"Oh yeah, it's okay. Say! Can you give me a ride over there?" Richard nodded towards the lighted arena.

"Heck, just taxi over there. It'll be okay." The farmer was very accomodating and his smile reassured Richard that it really was all right.

"Well, okay, if you say so." With that, Richard fired up and taxied through corn almost as high as the vertical stabilizer. The near-ripe ears banged on the leading edges of the wings, sounding like bullets. It was the fanciest corn picker in Kansas. Eventually, he came to the edge of the cornfield and parked. Richard reached in the back and grabbed his saddle, walked to the chutes, and placed third in the saddle bronc competition.

Well, like I said, there aren't too many ways to get to Burden. There's the road and then there's that path—the one through the tall corn.

# Fire Drill!
# (American Style)

Few things can instill terror like fire. The threat of a fire on an airplane can double—even triple—that terror. There are few ways to fight one and virtually nowhere to go to escape it, especially if airborne.

Consider the possibilities: A fire may begin in an engine compartment and spread to all that fuel. The loss of an engine is handicap enough. The loss of a wing is fatal. Because of this grim reality, emergency procedures have been written into every flight manual. In this case, we're talking about airline flight manuals. Those procedures are not included just to decorate the manuals to which they belong. Great amounts of time are devoted to them in flight simulator training and aircraft checkrides. So much time, in fact, is devoted to them that a fire warning in the cockpit will produce a predictable reaction from the crew. These predictable reactions can play into the hands of wise competitors.

Much has already been said about competition between various airlines. The management teams joust for productive routes and timely departures. Much of this is done in high office penthouses, far away from the whine and din of jet aircraft. The amazing part is how, upon the publishing of a new timetable, the competition has a matching schedule. If there is an answer to all this, it is espionage, pure and simple.

It is a war of sorts, and the objective is to capture the enemy's passengers.

Away from the quiet, posh offices with a potted plant in every corner marches the company's infantry—batallions of people who make every day a battle for customer supremacy. As a passenger, you're a pawn in this larger war. Of course, you have no choice on how much you will pay, which airline you will ride, or what time you will leave. But then, maybe the reason you arrived a few minutes late at your destination wasn't the airline's fault at all. It could have been something much deeper.

It could have been sabotage!

The airport is JFK in New York. The time is 6:00 P.M. a massive pushback is just beginning. Jets of every color and description are

72

whining and creeping into line, filling the arteries of the airport like so many colored corpuscles. Within that line, two airplanes have accidentally been paired. Both are bound for the same destination. They are direct competitors. It is an undeclared war in the trenches.

The plane in the lead is an American Airlines 727, lumbering along at the usual snail's pace, American's company trademark. At least that is the belief of those who most regularly follow them. Behind them is a Braniff flight, chomping at the bit. Braniff is in diametric opposition to American when it comes to taxi speed: Fast is usually not fast enough. Although the traffic would not allow a much faster taxi speed, the Braniff captain vows to beat American to the destination one way or another.

Eventually the procession halts short of the runway. The American flight is near the yellow hold line and ready for their clearance. Tower controllers are overworked at times like this and this fellow is talking about as fast as his brain and jaw muscles will allow.

"American 554, taxi into position and hold. Braniff 93, be ready to follow him and expect a vector for separation on departure."

These instructions were logical, but in no way fit the Braniff captain's plan for winning the race. The vector after takeoff would very nearly determine the outcome before they ever got started.

Turning to his first officer, the captain commanded: "Hit the fire bell warning test switch when I give you the word." The first officer was bewildered, but as with all good first officers, he immediately remembered Rule Number One, which is followed by Rule Number Two. (If you are not familiar with Rule Number 1 and Rule Number 2, we will take the time here to go over them. Rule Number 1: *The captain is always right.* Rule Number 2: *If the captain is wrong, see Rule Number 1.*)

The radio crackled: "American 554, cleared for takeoff. Braniff 93, position and hold."

The Braniff crew released the parking brake and rolled softly toward the runway. American brought the three-holer up to METO power and hustled down the runway. The Braniff captain was intent on American's takeoff roll. He reached down and gripped the mike.

"Hit the fire bell!" It was almost a bellow. The cockpit was alive with red lights and the clamor of the bell. Holding the microphone high in the air, he pressed the talk button. The sound pierced the airwaves and erupted through the speakers of the control tower and every cockpit on the frequency.

American 554 was midstream in takeoff, but below $V_1$

(takeoff speed). Predictably, the American captain retarded the thrust levers upon hearing the fire bell and reversed. Heading for the nearest high-speed taxiway, the takeoff was aborted.

"American 554, do you need the equipment?" the controller asked.

"Negative, we can't seem to find the problem." The crew was a bit perplexed.

"Roger; then taxi back and call ground. Braniff 93 is cleared for takeoff." In one breath the controller had the abnormality under control.

The Braniff captain was beside himself with his devious plan. Indeed, he would win this one, legal or not.

"Braniff 93 is rolling. Good day, ya'll."

# I'm Only in It for the Money

Those who have been to war know the stark terror that battle can bring. It's hard to believe in peacetime that there is a job that could bring that sort of terror into the heart of an aviator almost nightly.

There is a job like that, though: Flying cargo or mail in small airplanes, late at night, without radar, is that kind of job. If you find this statement hard to believe, then one of two things is true: Either you've never been in a thunderstorm, or you've never flown for a crummy outfit like I did.

At Great Western Airlines almost everything was a company oversight. An airplane with two wings was an oversight. The attitude was much like this:

"Hey, this is Griffin in Spokane. Say, did you know my airplane only has one wing?"

"One wing? You mean it's only got one wing?" The voice on the other end was incredulous.

"That's right," I smirked.

"Well, gee, uh, you flew it like that last night, didn't you?" he asked. Why are telephone conversations with company ops always like this? I was thinking, What's in this guy's coffee?

"Yeah, I flew it last night, but I assure you it had two wings!" I tapped the table with my index finger as I spoke. "Well, uh, Griff, let me check on it?" Good thing it's his nickel. There was a long time passing while I was on hold. He came back on the line:

"Yeah, Griffin? They say the wing has been removed. It's part of a company plan to facilitate quicker turnaround times. It seems someone figured out that with that wing removed, you can load and unload the plane a great deal quicker."

I had to be sarcastic: "Well, that certainly makes sense."

"Yeah, it kinda does, doesn't it? Well, we'll have it back on by tomorrow night. You can go back to the house." This guy has got to be kidding, I thought, but with this company, you never know.

So many things at Great Western weren't a joke. There were real honest-to-goodness screw-ups. One weekend I flew the plane to Reno for scheduled maintenance. Upon arrival I asked them where I was to stay. They said I was supposed to stay on some

guy's couch I'd never ever heard of before. I rented my own motel room.

Upon returning to the airport for the trip back to Spokane I preflighted the airplane. Everything looked good enough—good enough, that is, until I tried to taxi. The Aztec (which I called Azwreck) could not be maneuvered out of the parking spot between two other planes. It was in a tight spot, but surely my abilities as a pilot were not as meager as the Azwreck was making them seem.

After three minutes of jockeying engines back and forth, I got the airplane out and headed down a taxiway. I decided to investigate further. When the left toe brake was depressed, the plane would turn right, and vice versa. Now I knew the secret to maneuvering this plane.

Back to the maintenance hangar we went, pushing right to go left. It took our excellent mechanics only four hours to discover what they had done in the first place and then undo it.

Great Western 612 was an accident looking for a place to happen. The engines were never right. Every night's flight was an exercise in self-control—the kind that soldiers practice during a firefight. I'm not kidding. Up the Salmon River and Hell's Canyon there are extremely few places that one could safely land in an emergency. Nightfall makes the odds of successfully completing a forced landing one in a billion. Thus, a forced landing, to me, meant sure death.

Getting myself ready for each night's flight was an incredible psyching process. It usually began around 5:30 P.M., when I would sit down in front of the TV and wait for the weather forecast during the news. Usually, it was less than a beautiful forecast. Storms or ice were standard ingredients, draped over tons of sawtoothed mountains.

Information like that just about always got my juices flowing. For the next three hours I'd sit on the end of the couch— thinking, reflecting, and watching my knuckles turn white. At the stroke of 8:30 it was time to leave for the airport. The psyching process would end as I'd run to the car, screaming *Banzai!*

More than once I arrived to find that ragged old Aztec in pieces on the hangar floor. Such was not the case this night. She sat perched on her sturdy legs, ready to go. Two hours later we were in Boise, fueling and loading for the trip back. The flight down had been the usual agony of not knowing whether we would reach altitude before the mountains would reach up and tickle our belly. Infernal clouds were obscuring all the peaks along the route. The flight back would entail more of the same.

Luckily, when leaving Boise the airway follows the Salmon river and the terrain does not rise as quickly as the southbound flight.

The old Aztec struggled to the 12,000-foot mark. I had her Rajay turbochargers wide open for every ounce of horsepower and, once there, she flew along easily. Just the same, some of the Pacific Northwest's harshest country was only a few thousand feet below. On every flight from Boise, the point I lived for was the changeover between Salt Lake Center and Seattle Center. The reason this meant so much to me was that it occurred directly over Hell's Canyon. Going northbound it meant a lower altitude and the beginning of the correlative descent into Lewiston. The highest terrain is on the south side of Hell's Canyon, the Seven Devils range. At that point the mountain peaks are only 2,000 feet below the plane flying at the minimum enroute altitude (MEA) of 12,000 feet. There isn't much room for altitude loss.

Anyway, the old wreck and I had been flying along for about 45 minutes. We hadn't seen the ground since Boise. Then, instantly, terror gripped me. The right engine just spooled down to about 20 percent power. My engine-out procedures were automatic. It was a good thing, because the thinking side of my brain was hailed by panic. I threw all the levers forward—props, throttles, and mixtures—and stopped. I kept thinking, "My God, they haven't called me to change over. The Seven Devils have got to be straight ahead. I'm losing altitude!" In all this panic, my subconscious was doing all the necessary work. Flashes kept creeping in like, "The engine still has about 20 percent power; do I kill it? Is 20 percent better than a feathered prop?"

Then, like curtains blowing in a breeze before a storm, the flashes would cover my brain in panic: "I've got to tell somebody, get some help. My God, I'm going to die. This is really it! I'm going to die in the hands of this bitter old wreck!" I gripped the microphone, scared to key it. I wanted to sound professional, but the controller called instead.

"Great Western 612, contact Seattle 128.15." It was the most beautiful message ever. I looked at the altimeter. We had lost three hundred feet so far, but we were across Hell's Canyon.

All I could muster was a "Roger." Then I switched the radio. "Seattle, Great Western 612, level 12,000." I lied; we were really at 11,700. "Sure could use lower," I continued. The engine was still gagging.

"Well, descend and maintain 10,500." It was glorious. We could make Lewiston, more than likely. Then, as if Murphy's Law had been repealed, the engine caught and began to run as strong as the other one. It never missed a lick the rest of the night and I flew back to Spokane. As it turned out, not feathering it *was* the correct thing to do.

After landing at Spokane, I called the company and reported the mechanical problem. It was business as usual.

"You lost an engine? How'd you make it back? Most of the guys don't make it back, you know—cause the other engine ain't no good either." Is this guy kidding? I mean, come on, this place is just too flaky.

"Well, yeah, I made it back, you idiot. All I've got to say is get somebody to look at it before tomorrow night. Goodbye." I was peeved.

The psyching process began early the next night. I kept wondering if they got someone to look at that engine. As usual, the weather was lousy with ice and clouds. I sat, hanging on to the arm of the couch, for a long time. Finally, 8:30 P.M. came. "Banzaiiii . . .!" I was off to the war again.

There she was, sitting just as I left her. She had a cunning smile. I don't care if the mechanic did say that all they found were fouled plugs, she still looked like she was going to try to stick me in the mountains. The job was getting to be a classic struggle—a triangle, if you wish: man against machine, man against the element, and machine against the elements. Nothing pulled together. It was strictly one pitted against the others.

Not to be slighted was my inner conflict: *Why am I doing this? Is it the love of flying? Is it the adventure and danger? Could it be the money? Naw, this is aviation; there ain't no money here.* But, I decided, should anyone ask, that's what I'll tell them: "I'm only in it for the money."

We made it back to Hell's Canyon that night without a hitch. The weather wasn't any better, but the engine seemed to be holding out. We busted out of the clouds over the Snake and I could see Lewiston ahead. "It's all downhill from here," I thought. Good thinking. The engine gagged and choked. It was startling, completely unexpected, but with the lights of Lewiston ahead it wasn't as unnerving this time. From experience, I waited for the engine to regain power as it did on final approach.

Again I flew the crate to Spokane without further problem. It was back to the phone: "This is Griffin in Spokane. That airplane is not fixed. She lost power on me again going into Lewiston."

The response was predictable: "She lost power on you, huh?"

I didn't wait for the rest of the schtick. "Listen, you tell whoever you are supposed to tell that if that airplane isn't fixed by tomorrow night, find another pilot!"

Now, as a writer, I realize that this story could have ended after the first engine failure and been enough. The truth, though, demands that the entire saga of the Azwreck's affliction be told.

The mechanics looked after the worn engine all the next day. They replaced plugs and magnetos and for several weeks there were no more engine failures. Still, the engine was not copacetic.

The flight down from Spokane to Lewiston was always serene. Generally, the rippled hills left by the currents of some ancient sea were locked in the mauve and violent shadows of twilight. Dropping over the cliffs at White Bird Hill was the most exhilarating part of any summer's evening. So close to the hill, sometimes that I thought the tail would surely drag on the cliffs behind. It was a roller coaster ride, a plunge of several thousand feet. At the end of the slide lay the runway—convenient, yet all part of the fun.

As 56 Yankee slid through the flare the right engine did its number. When the power was brought to idle to touch down, the prop went to feather. It stopped so quickly it looked like a policeman raising his hand to halt traffic. Fortunately, the loss of power happened so late in the landing there were no directional control problems.

During the turnaround I checked the oil, thinking that lack of oil caused the prop to feather. It was full; moreover, the engine swung right to life on taxi-out. Southbound to Boise we went, up and over the mountains. For crying out loud, this job was starting to give me ulcers. For the next several days, two out of every three landings ended with a feathered prop.

At this point you're probably wondering why I didn't have it fixed. Believe me, I complained, and daily they tried different remedies to no avail. Finally, a friend from Texas came to visit and I asked him if he'd like to ride along one night. Being a new private pilot, he was ecstatic to be able to fly in a twin-engine plane.

On the first landing into Lewiston, the prop stood straight up. Calvin about lost his choppers pointing at the dead engine. "Eh, that's all right. It does that all the time. Don't worry about it." I was nonchalant and indifferent about the problem now. Great Western had a way of making a conscientious pilot numb.

Calvin was worrisome, as any intelligent human being would have been: "You don't *really* think that engine is all right do you?"

"Well, not really, but no one can figure out what's wrong with it.

As long at it keeps turning between takeoff and landing, it doesn't really concern me. After all, *I'm only in this for the money*." It was spoken in true air mail pilot's manner. I hoped that Calvin was consoled, but I doubted it.

Leg by leg, we completed the trip with the engine sputtering to a stop during each flare. At trip's end, Calvin was as used to it stopping as I was. We went home and retired to a cozy bed.

The next evening came early and my psyching process was short due to our house guests. "Banzaiii . . . !" And off I went.

The Cappels turned to my wife and asked, "Does he always do that?"

"Fraid so. I think he's nuts."

The arrival at the airport was strange and mystifying. The Azwreck was nowhere in sight. Things began to go through my head: *Maybe I'm fired 'cause I told them I wouldn't fly it anymore.* I looked inside the hangar where they usually worked on it—no 56Y. I walked down to the next hangar. She wasn't there either. On the way back to the car I walked back through the first hangar. There was a big canvas partition around one corner of the hangar. Moving the canvas aside like a little boy sneaking into a circus, I peered into the dimly lit area.

There she was. They must have been embarrassed that they were working on such a wreck. She was in thousand pieces, raised up on jacks. I wouldn't be flying *this* airplane for a while.

It was time to call Operations. "Say, this is Griffin in Spokane. What's going on with my plane?" It seemed like all my conversations with Tulsa started like this.

"What do you mean?" He was as informed as usual.

"Well, she's in a million pieces in a dark hangar and not a soul around." Don't these guys know *anything* that's going on?

"Oh, yeah, uh, she's got a blown jug," he responded. "An AD note came out on the engine mounts and while they were checking them they found it had a blown jug."

"I can't believe it. For a month they've been trying to find out what is wrong with the damn thing and during a check of the *engine mounts* they find a blown jug? Do you get the feeling they really don't really know what the hell they're doing?" I knew I was asking the wrong person, so I didn't give him a chance to answer. "So what do you want me to do tonight?" I was figuring they'd come up with something neat—like fly the route in a 172.

"Take the night off. She'll be ready for next week. We'll call you." He was as reassuring as could be expected.

"This won't cost me any pay, will it?" I wanted to cover the important things. With an outfit like this, you never knew.

"Nope; won't cost you a thing," he came back in his best "great news" voice.

"Great! Cause you know *I'm only in this for the money!*" And then I thought to myself, "There may not be that much money in the world."

# Cool under Pressure

There are probably a few million stories about flight attendants that are told and retold daily. We'll probably go through several more before the end of the book. Some stories illustrate the naivete of a flight attendant, some the ingenuity, and some the calm, cool reaction when a tight situation demands it.

There's no good place to have a heart attack, but believe me, to have one on an airplane is the ultimate franchise of Murphy's Law. It happens more often than you would think. For example, we've had at least two at our airline in the last two years. Three years ago, I was on a Delta flight that got priority ATC handling due to a heart attack victim. Not long ago, I heard another Delta flight going into Dallas with the same problem. I don't know what Delta does; maybe it's just that they handle such a large number of people that the odds are against them. It is obvious, nonetheless, that heart attacks do occasionally happen in flight.

The flight was on a Shorts SD3-30 between Wichita Falls, Texas, and Dallas-Fort Worth. For Vicki, the flight attendant, it was like so many others: Climb to altitude, serve drinks, and take care of the guy with horrendous chest pains.

It was during the descent that a passenger rang for Vicki's assistance. "Say, this guy's leaning on me. I think something's wrong with him."

He looked bad. Vicki didn't know exactly what was wrong with him, but something bad was wrong with him for sure. She reached down and loosened his tie. He was still breathing, but it was shallow.

"See if you can get him into the aisle and lay him down while I go tell the Captain," she said to the passenger who was sitting next to the victim. A couple of guys got up and got him out in the aisle. Meanwhile, the flight crew got priority handling into Dallas and called for the paramedics.

It took only a short time to reach the airport, during which Vicki attended to the victim's requirements. It was like saving lives was an everyday activity for her. (Some days on Metro seem that way.) As soon as the parking brake was set, the paramedics

were on the airplane to assist. The other passengers filed off quickly to give the medics more room to work. Vicki's job was done.

In true feminine fashion, she went to the lavatory to check her makeup and hair. The heart attack victim was still spread out in the aisle with paramedics working feverishly to maintain his life signs. It was at that point that Chris Cofield came out of the cockpit and went to the rear to get the refueling started. In the midst of this poor gentleman's life-or-death crisis, Chris passed Vicki. With the victim virtually at her feet she asked, "Chris, does my hair look all right? Do I need more lipstick?"

Chris could scarcely believe his ears. But then, that's Vicki—cool under pressure.

Maybe *too* cool?

# What Time Is It, Really?

Some airlines get reputations they don't deserve. Almost all are very good. In fact, U.S. airlines are the best in the world for comfort and courteousness. Nonetheless, out of these various reputations come a few gems. This story is a classic and we don't know if it's true or just folklore, but it is amusing.

The afternoon rush hour is much the same at any hub airport, and St. Louis is a hub. Many airlines fly in and out, carrying with them their various notorieties. As can be expected, air traffic controllers are aware of the reputations, and—to a certain extent—each airline has a "flying personality."

The airwaves were full of instructions: Turn left; Turn right; Descend to . . . Each aircraft acknowledged each new instruction and the chatter was constant.

All at once there was silence. The controller had all his pieces in place.

The silence was broken by an unknown voice: "What time is it?"

The controller came back with this now-famous retort: "Well, it depends on who wants to know. If that's American asking, it's 1700 local. If that's United, then it's 2200 Zulu. If it's Ozark, Mickey's little hand is on the five!"

# The Ultralight Experience

Ultralight airplanes are the future of general aviation. That's what I was thinking when I bought a dealership to sell these fun machines—not to mention making a lot of money.

My experience with them since has convinced me of several things. First, the most dangerous business proposition in the world is to sell something that you are in love with—in this case, airplanes. You cannot assume that because you love your product, anyone else will.

The second thing I found out was that everyone thinks ultralight airplanes are great, but nobody is going to put money into one because of his ideals. They have to want one *very* badly.

And the third thing I found out was that no one is going to test fly the airplane after repair but me.

Most of the articles—maybe 100 percent—that I have seen written about ultralights sing the high praises of the idea. Most pilot/authors believe (as I did) that ultralights are the wave upon which the future of aviation rides. This may very well be the truth. However, after my experience with these machines I see them as a stepping stone to larger, more dependable (ergo, more stable) airplanes.

A pilot of many thousands of hours can get caught short of flying ideas in an ultralight. In fact, my experience in heavier airplanes, some say, might have been a hindrance. I doubt that seriously! Let me relate a few of my adventures. It will be a biased point of view, granted. Perhaps, though, if you are considering an ultralight airplane, it could save you some grief.

Now, I'm not going to mention the manufacturer's name of my chosen dealership. Suffice it to say that it was one of the top three or four selling brands—one that has two seats. Also, we will talk only about flying experiences and not the fiasco of dealing with a manufacturer that has gotten too big, too fast.

Flying any airplane comes naturally after several thousand hours. One comes to expect an airplane to react in various ways to various control inputs and atmospheric conditions. Indeed, the ultralight will fly like an airplane. The rub comes when

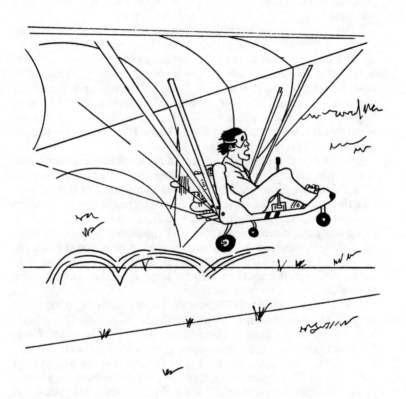

anything is askew or the least bit out of line. When that happens, an ultralight behaves badly—*very* badly.

No one with good sense learns to fly an experimental aircraft without first learning to taxi, then doing short hops, and finally an all-out flight. That's how I went about it. However, a problem that is easily controllable and compensated for in an ultralight flying in ground effect is difficult (at best) in the air, away from the ground. The problem, whatever it might be, is masked by the ground effect. It doesn't really show up until the airplane is well airborne.

My first problem with the machine was one of abrupt pitch-up. In ground effect, the problem was hardly noticeable. In the air, the problem was severe. When the engine was brought back to idle, the airplane would do the opposite of the expected: The nose would pitch skyward as if I had *added* power in a normal airplane—a great deal of power. (Remember, all this was happening during one flight.) Well, I thought, that's easy enough to correct for; when I reduce power I'll add forward stick—simple solution to a simple problem.

The normal reaction to expect of an airplane in a turn is for the nose to pitch down, for the airplane to lose lift. *Not so,* said this aluminum monster. The nose will pitch up. For a pilot who has flown the last ten years in airplanes, that one reaction goes against the flow. It is a particularly difficult game of reprogramming one's mind and hands to do the opposite of what they have been programmed to do. The experience of past years paid off, however, in the seat of the pants. Although the airplane was doing different things than other planes, I could feel everything it was doing and correct for it.

The trouble with this flight was that my skill (bag of tricks, if you will) was not enough. I was flying out of a 500-foot long field. There were power lines at one end and houses at the other. Now, 500 feet is long enough for an ultralight, even with obstacles like that, but it takes skill. My first time around, I came in just over the wires and chopped the power. As predicted, the nose started up, so I pushed forward on the stick. Even so, the glide turned out to be too long. The field slipped by before the wheels were even close to the grass. Around we went. This time I'd be sure to get down in time.

On final approach I set up a long way out. The wires were hard to see in the early morning light, but I knew they were there. *Whoops,* looks like I'm below them. I added power and climbed to just clear them. The power was chopped and a good deal of forward stick was added. The plane started into what appeared to be a fairly good glide. I concentrated on how much field was left, neglecting the airspeed indicator. It looked like we'd touch down just halfway down.

Suddenly we were a parachute. She just stopped flying. My thoughts started racing as I observed the stalled condition we were in. The ground looks distant even when it's only seven or eight feet below.

My thoughts raced on: "Looks like it's gonna be a hard landing. No time to recover, no altitude, and the engine's coughing. Maybe she'll fly when we get in ground effect. Is there anything left?" I pulled the stick back just before impact. "Ugh, that's a hard landing!" The plane bounced and then dug its nose into the dirt. The world started moving around the plane, or maybe . . . no maybe. We were flipping over! As I had heard so many times before, everything went into slow motion.

The thought of bending an airplane appalled me. How could I be so stupid. I was a high-time pilot and had never even scratched a plane. Yet here I was in the process of totalling-out the first airplane I had ever owned.

My thoughts continued: "So this is what it feels like to flip an airplane or car. She is stopped and I'm still alive. I bet I look *real* stupid hanging here upside down in this damn thing."

I could see my neighbor walking up to see if I was all right. As I dropped out of my inverted perch, I commented that I was okay, but the airplane was a mess. Several neighbors helped me pull the wreckage back home from the flying field down the street.

Since I was a dealer, the repairs only cost me about $580. Someone else would have paid nearly $800. My first thoughts were to repair and get out of the business. I should have. Yet the pilot in me was saying that I couldn't let an airplane defeat me.

After talking with the manufacturer, we decided that what we were dealing with was a weight-and-balance problem. After all, it couldn't be a trim problem. The plane was built and flown for over 20 hours at the factory; certainly all the bugs had been worked out of it—another false assumption.

So, came time for me to get back up on the horse that threw me. With a hundred-pound bag of molding plaster in the other seat, the balance should be in my favor.

The plan that morning was to take off from the neighborhood field and fly to a grass airport where I had rented an open hangar. (During the process of rebuilding, the airplane had been wind-damaged in my front yard.) The idea was that there would be more than enough room to learn to fly this monstrosity out at the country airport. I wasn't going to gamble on trying to land the airplane in 500 feet until I was *real* good at it. Therefore, when the plane was airborne, we weren't stopping unitl we got to Hilltop Airport.

Confident that the 100-pound bag of ballast had taken care of my problems, we taxied to the end of the field and did a short hop. Like I said before, you can't tell that much about handling characteristics while flying in ground effect. Once airborne, for good, it was apparent that the problem was as bad as ever. The flight to Hilltop was the longest flight of my life. It had to be the longest 20 minutes on record.

First my arm gave out from holding forward pressure. (There were no mechanical trim tabs.) Next, I was literally having to sit on the edge of my seat to trim the airplane forward at all. Friends, we might have only been 400 or 500 feet in the air, but there is *nothing* between the seat and the ground. You can look right between your legs for an unobstructed view of earth below. If flying helped you overcome your fear of heights, this is sure to give it back to you.

Next, the engine began to miss a stroke or two—just a few at first, but by the end of the flight it was missing about a third of the time. If anyone has said that ultralights will glide well without an engine, then he has never flown a *real* airplane, or he has been practicing with rocks. Believe me, they glide worse than the all-time version of a flying rock, the Piper Tri-Pacer. When the engine quits, it's Elevator City. Sure, the plane is flying and not stalling. Its chosen place to land, however, is not likely to agree with yours.

Hilltop was in sight only about a mile and a half ahead. A lot of trees were also ahead that were reaching up at me and the green monster. I was scared to death. The airplane was trying to pitch up against full forward stick. I had no more control to the forward end left and I knew that if the engine quit altogether she was going to pitch up. That meant a stall and no forward stick. The prospects made me nauseous.

Lord, I wanted on the ground. My body was aching from the position I was having to sit in. Finally, the grass runway slid up underneath the airplane. I kept about half power on and forced her to the ground. At the flare, I cut the engine. She pitched up and landed herself. As she rolled to a stop I leaned back for the first time in about 20 minutes. Death and gravity had been cheated once again—no small feat this time.

That should have been it for me and ultralights. The challenge, though, still beckoned. A friend of mine and I talked about it for quite a while. The airplane had to be trimmed; that's all there was to it. It simply could not be flown again until that problem was remedied. A phone call back to the factory proved what had been obvious: The angle of incidence of the horizontal stabilizer had to be changed to trim the plane. The question in my mind was this: They flew it at the factory. Did they fly it like this? I was fed up with the company. They don't know apple butter from . . . well, you know what I mean. Maybe I could ignore them and pretend I designed this airplane and stop listening to their shenanigans.

With the trim situation well in hand, the ultralight began to fly like a normal apparatus of the air. Of course,we had to repair and ignore the occasional wind damage. (They are *so* fragile.) After a few outings it became possible for me to take people up to enjoy the wonders of ultralight flight.

Finally, when my wife, Debi, got to go along, the green monster chose to break again. In the midst of a trip around the pattern, the monster began to vibrate uncomfortably. It was *extremely* disconcerting. Perhaps it was the prop, or that bearing on the propeller shaft. At any rate, we couldn't get around the pattern quick enough.

Again on solid ground, I was finally realizing that although ultralight airplanes must be for *somebody,* they didn't seem to be for *me.* An airplane that had less than two of my own hours on it had been broken and required at least 80 hours of work so far. Forty to one is *not* what I call reliability.

The bearing was the problem. We replaced it and went for a test flight. A friend and I took off. About a quarter of the way around the pattern it was apparent that we had climbed all that we could climb. As a matter of fact, we began to descend. I picked a cow pasture for landing spot; we'd never make it back to the runway. But she hung in there. I cut the pattern short and we barely cleared the hill from which Hilltop gets its name.

A close inspection revealed that the bearing bracket was slightly larger than the worn-out one we had replaced. That one factor caused the propeller shaft to be out of line and the drive belt to walk up the sprocket to a binding position—only a *slight* bind, mind you, but enough to reduce horsepower below that needed for two individuals.

The cold sweat had barely dried from my hands a few days later when Debi got a call from the airport operator. It seems that strong south winds preceeding a cold front had damaged the monster. He said it wasn't bad, but inspection showed it to be major. A new kingpost was necessary to put the thing back in the air.

That was it. We threw in the towel. The business account that we started was close to being out of money. When the kingpost gets here, we'll repair the plane. The sprockets need to be aligned, and then it's for sale.

Any takers?

# Like Walking on Water

Have you ever wondered why Visual Approach Slope Indicators were invented? Well, I wondered for a long time. Most of my flying experience had been in the flatlands of the South. Snow was not usually a consideration, and the slope of a runway was not a factor either. When I moved to the mountains it became obvious that the VASI was a useful tool. It really was indispensable at some of the fields, as I found out.

The effect of a sloped runway is complicated in the winter, as I witnessed one snowy morning. The weather was improving at the destination. Light snow had been falling all night, turning the mountains and valleys into Christmas card scenes. The peaks were all hidden in the low clouds, but the visibility was generally three to five miles except in the snow showers. There was no way to fly VFR that morning, so we saddled up and took off IFR.

The flight progressed routinely. We changed frequencies, chatted with the controllers, and finally were cleared for the approach. The VOR approach had low enough minimums for the weather, so there was no concern that I would not see the airport.

Little did I know that while I was completing the procedure turn, the snowplow was finishing his last swath on the runway. As he turned around to head for the barn, he clipped the VASI installation with the blade. The VASI was out.

Like every good instrument pilot should, we descended to the MDA as quickly as possible. We broke out early and, of course, the MDA had us low. The usual technique is to fly along level until intercepting the glideslope on the VASI, then follow it down to the runway. The new snow blanketed everything in sight. The world looked white and the runway was out there somewhere straight ahead.

Finally, we spotted the hangars and could make out the runway. It was snow-packed and no sand had been put out. That would have helped with depth perception. As it was, my depth perception was nil. Looking for the VASI, we found two boxes

protruding out of the snow and that was it. I set up for the approach normally.

As we got closer to the runway, I noticed the need for more power—then a *lot* more power. We touched down in the first ten feet of plowed runway and rolled quickly to a stop. Looking straight ahead, I could see plainly that the runway was sloping up. Though I often flew into the airport, I always used the VASI and never really thought about the slope. The bad depth perception, coupled with the illusion created by the sloping runway—not to mention starting low from the MDA in the first place—was enough to threaten to ruin a good pilot and his family.

While we were in the lobby, the snowplow driver walked in. He was not aware that he'd hit the VASI yet, but he had seen our approach.

"Say, are you the pilot who just flew in?" he asked.

"Yes, I am."

"Boy, you're pretty good. Your wheels just skimmed the snow the last 25 yards to the runway. Ain't never seen anything like that. Kinda like Jesus walking on the water." He was impressed. He turned away to talk to his boss.

I thought to myself, "Like Jesus walking on the water, huh? I could have been killed out there. If it hadn't have been for God being my copilot, our bones might be getting rather cool by now."

# Doing It Backwards

So much of today's flying is cut-and-dried. You take off, fly a little while, and finish with an instrument approach that is successful. As for missed approaches, they are few and far between. A missed approach always has a way to introduce a small element of surprise and put a sense of adventure back into a flight. Anything out of the ordinary is usually remembered for a long time, just because it *is* different. Such was the case on a winter evening several years ago.

Captain William (Billy) Ehl was at the controls. He performed what had to be the most difficult and precarious approach I have ever seen. Fog was the culprit this night, and even though the landing runway was ILS-equipped, it was the pilot's skill that brought the flight to a safe conclusion. Sitting in the jump seat, I had the bird's eye view of the entire spectacle.

The situation was an odd one. The visibility was being reported as a half mile and the ceiling as indefinite 100 feet. From our vantage point approaching the airport, it became evident the weather looked different from ground than from the air. The truth was, there *was* no ceiling! Stars adorned the night, surrounding the plane. The fog was only a thin layer in much the same manner that silt covers the bottom of a beautiful lake.

The fog reached from what seemed about 200 feet down to the ground. As we flew over, the lights on the ground were perfectly visible. They seemed to just invite us home. Looking far ahead, toward the airport, it was like a battle. The airport beacon swept through the fog like a laser. The sequenced flashers exploded in the fog like depth charges detonating beneath a glassy sea.

As we started down the glide path, it became clear that we wouldn't reach the misty envelope until the decision height. What a decision! Finally, we descended to decision altitude. The lights were all there, lighting the fog up like the Las Vegas strip.

Well, the rules say that if you have the runway environment in sight, it is legal to land. Sure enough, we were legal all right, but this was instrument flying in reverse. Aren't the visibility conditions supposed to *improve* at the DH on an approach in minimum weather? Not tonight. They got *worse*—certainly, a situation where the pilot must adapt quickly if safety is to be assured.

Thinking back on that night, it becomes apparent there is precious little in any pilot's training or experience to make that task easier. On a runway without VASI such as this one, the only technique had to be one of rapid alternating between the dismal, misty, almost mirage-like visual references, and the flight instruments on the panel. But Billy was (and is) a highly experienced pilot and was up to the task that night. Deftly he followed the glideslope down until the strobes were behind him. Then, upon reaching an altitude of near 50 feet, he relied upon the runway lights for course guidance and depth perception. Possibly he monitored the VSI for a shallow rate of descent. At last the wheels squeaked in agreement to a job well done. Slowly, we taxied to the terminal through the murk.

Experience probably had everything to do with the success of that approach. Yet it would be unusual if a pilot had ever seen that same situation before. It may only happen once in every 10,000 hours of flying. Two or three times might be all a pilot would experience it in a career.

Unquestionably, the first time around with it *is* an *experience!*

# Just Like the Days of Old

In days gone by radar was an unknown quantity. Airborne weather radar was especially rare. Organized Air Traffic Control as we know it today did not even begin to evolve until 1956. It took many years before Air Traffic Control radar was commonplace in most sections of the United States.

The pilots who flew the skies prior to that time were truly pioneers of the air. They were men who fought the battles of weather and schedule with sketchy weather information at best. Time occasionally reverts back to that kind of flying though it happens more rarely in the 1980s. The reason for this is that regulations require radar in more airplanes that fly for commercial reasons. Also, the reliability of the ATC computer system is being updated and upgraded. All this is not to forget that Air Route Traffic Control Centers are having weather radar installed along with their narrow band traffic radar.

However, every now and then things dissolve all the electronic barriers that keep us safe from the storms and a pilot is called upon to make a flight relying on his experience, wits, and instinct.

Early in my flying career I got a taste of what flying was like "in the good old days." The plane was an old Beech 18. It was probably as old as I was. The only good thing about the plane was that it had been retrofitted with PT-6 turbine engines and we were a little dubious as to how good those were. The plane was much like to an old lady trying to look young and not quite making it. Nevertheless, it was a job, and one that I have been thankful for having many times.

It was to be one of the most nerve-wracking experiences of my entire career, even up to this day. A line of thunderstorms had been plaguing us all week. Every time we came up against them they seemed to have gotten a little worse. Maybe it's just that they were wearing us down. They were associated with a slow-moving cold front and we had to cross it back-to-front, then, on the return, front-to-back each night of this particular work week. Having been through the line several times already didn't make my captain and I relish the task. We'd been belittled, angered, and beaten by this string of storms to the point that we were considering resigning and going into another line of work.

The Beech Turbine 18 was droning towards Chicago inbound from Pittsburgh and the brilliant lightning display ahead was testimony of what was to come. It was about 4:00 in the morning and we were tired as always. The flashing stung our eyes and one of Chicago Center's finest stung us as well. The controller said the line was 40 to 60 miles thick and was solid for 120 miles in either direction from us. The line was massive in length as well as depth. We had no onboard radar and the controller was as much help.

"Great Western 658, what I'm painting is solid and I see no holes."

We queried further: "Is *anyone* going through *anywhere?*"

"I haven't had anybody try it in a couple of hours."

"Which way looks the best from here?"

"It all looks bad; I have no suggestions. You are free to deviate any direction you wish."

Great, no radar help of any kind and the look on the captain's face told me we were going to put our nose into it anyway. Soon he gave me instructions to watch for lightning pulses and said that we would veer away from areas of greatest intensity and most flashes.

It was odd in that normally we descended to 4,000 feet to get ready for the ride. Tonight was different. I guess it was instinct, because there certainly was no visual information suggesting that our 6,000 feet was the altitude we should use. The hair was standing up on the back of my neck as we came abeam of a storm on each side—electricity, and it was close.

A stratus deck began to slide underneath us and seconds later we were safely past the two huge columns of cloud. The scene inside the line was eerie. We were enveloped by clouds above, below and alongside. In essence, it was like driving down a hallway or a boulevard lined with large trees. The lightning was making the trip more like a show in a laserium. Every time it would flash, we'd discuss whether it was cloud-to-cloud or a cell shooting its electrical messages to the ground. The cells weren't easily identified the way the lightning was bouncing around in that ball of clouds.

The controller, with all of his help, finally told us we had about another 20 miles to go. We veered this way until we saw a cell in front of us, then veered that way to miss seemingly countless masses of sullen, belly-swollen demons. The old 18 was still between layers and droning along contentedly. Her nonchalance seemed to say that she'd seen all this before. Her copilot

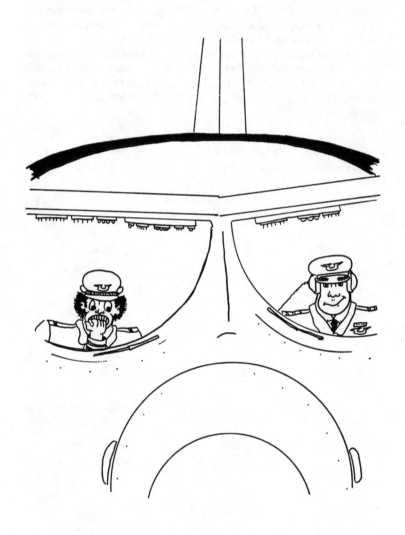

*hadn't.* The last 20 miles disappeared behind us and the constant flashing gave way to the steady glow of Chicago's millions, freshly washed to start a new day.

Looking over at the captain, it was easy to see the amazement on his face. The stern, straight-ahead, all-business gaze was gone and the twinkle in his eyes said it all. Neither of us could believe that we'd just flown 60 miles of nature's worst and never hit a ripple. Not a bump! The ride was satiny smooth. That's got to be some sort of near-psychic feat.

Certainly, I don't recommend use of this sort of technique. Yet, in the early days of aviation, that was the only way to do it. As it stands, I wouldn't want to go back into those same clouds again. But I wouldn't have missed this flight for anything in the world.

# Christmas in Puerto Rico

The sun had been gone from the sky for several hours. The night was becoming late and for the crew it had begun to get long. The old Convair stood on the ramp while the wind whistled around her legs. Inside the warm plane, Donna was stocking the galley and making fresh coffee for the load of troops that was about to get on. They would be chilled in the short walk from the terminal door to the airplane, with the temperature in the teens and the wind chill factor below zero.

The army sends home lots of troops at Christmas time—all they can spare. So it is not that unusual for an airline to fill up a plane with nothing but military personnel. As the men began to come aboard, it became evident to Donna that these weren't the ordinary brand of military men that she was used to seeing. All of them were Puerto Ricans. It wasn't a few here and a few there, but 50 Puerto Rican soldiers who understood very little English.

Donna is a black girl, a very outspoken and unprecautious woman. There isn't much that will get by her. Her speech is always full of zingers, and she is careful to never give a sucker an even break, as W.C. Fields put it. Captain Norton was a good match for her, with a wit at least as sharp. He noticed the Puerto Rican soldiers boarding the flight and made a mental note.

As wise as Donna is, she still doesn't get her full credit. As the soldiers were taking their seats for the flight, Donna walked down the aisle putting bags under the seat and removing all but clothing articles from the overhead rack. More than a couple of these young men noticed that Donna was very attractive and shapely and commented to each other as they watched her bend and stretch. Of course, the comments were made in Spanish, and the soldiers didn't think that she could understand.

But, like I said, Donna has a lot more going for her than she gets credit for. She is able to speak both German and Spanish. At first she took the comments as a compliment. However, as the comments continued, they began to sound more like propositions. Finally, one unsuspecting soul said the wrong thing—in Spanish, of course. Donna let loose, also in Spanish, "All right, sucker, keep your thoughts to yourself or I'll have you thrown off this plane!" He was shocked that she had understood him and was put squarely in his place.

Boot camp has never been a pleasant experience. Most soldiers can't wait to never see that place again. The mere thought of having to return to a hell hole like basic training creates deep depression in the heart of even the staunchest soldier. Captain Norton knew this. He also knew that these fellows spoke very little English. Whatever he said to these guys would have to be spoken in the manner of a drill sergeant if they were to understand.

Meanwhile, the flight had begun and the soldiers were confident that they were winging their way towards the warmer climes of Puerto Rico. Santa would be wearing bermuda shorts down there. To them it felt good to be going home.

By now Donna had served about half the cabin. Captain Norman came on the PA: "Good evening, gentlemen. Did I hear someone say they wanted to go back to Ft. Sill?" The cabin was thrown into instant pandemonium. Recently passed-out drinks were thrown into the air in a barrage of Cokes, coffee, and ice.

Donna was standing in the companionway near the main door. She was run over by five or six soldiers as they ran for the door. They began beating on the door and yelling, in English this time, "No no, no, no, no, we not go back to Ft. Sill!" They were determined to get off—in mid-air.

What just moments before had been a serene late-evening flight became chaos. Donna began wedging herself between the soldiers and the door. God only knows what would have happened if they had figured out how to open that door. In Spanish, she began hollering at the Puerto Ricans.

"We're not going back to Ft. Sill. It's a joke! The captain is a prankster! We're not going back to Ft. Sill. Please, sit down!" She was pleading. Eventually, she calmed them down and got everyone back in their seat.

In the cockpit, Captain Norton was chatting with his first officer as the plane pierced the night. Unaware of the level of chaos he had caused in the rear, he was sedate as usual. The cockpit door swung open and the light from the cabin cast the red light of the cockpit aside. It was Donna, of course, thoroughly convinced that she could commit murder upon her captain.

"Do you know what your smart . . . never mind. If you ever do that again, I'll kill you! I swear it!"

Captain Norton turned to his first officer as the cockpit door slammed shut. "Gee, do you think it was something I said?"

# Noise Abatement Procedure Number One

There is no end to the funny things a pilot hears on the radio. Although controllers seem to be a serious lot, they have their humorous moments. It isn't easy to be amusing under the restrained conditions in which they work. Nonetheless, one fellow had mastered the art of being funny and serious at the same time, perfectly.

*Controller:* "United 615, turn right 30 degrees for noise abatement."

*United 615:* "Uh, sir, we're level at 35,000 feet. What sort of noise abatement are you talking about?"

*Controller:* "Oh, the kind of noise that a United 727 will make when it meets a Western 737 at 500 miles an hour."

*United 615:* "Roger, turning right 30 degrees."

# The Scarlet Rose

Some mornings dawn magically. It's almost as if they have been brought down from heaven. This was one of those mornings as each crystal drop of dew sparkled in the growing light and the feel of a long-deserved spring was in the air. The air was musky with the scent of the year's first wildflowers.

Certainly, the old grass airport had never looked more beautiful than this morning, Grant thought, as he walked toward the office in the corner of the hangar.

"Hi, Ana, ready to go flyin'?" Grant spoke as he swung the door to the office open.

"You better believe I am. And it's such a beautiful morning, isn't it?" She was eager.

Grant thought to himself about how lucky he was to have such a great looking student. Students in general were rare in the days following the Crash of 29, much less female students. He filed through his drawer and found her progress folder. Then he briefly described the lesson's activities.

"Well, let's go fly," he proclaimed as he stood up. He towered over her, being well over six feet tall. Ana reached out for his extended hand as he helped her from her seat.

Out the hangar door and into the sun they walked casually toward the old yellow and blue biplane. Actually, it was about the only airplane on the field in those days, as Grant and his family had to sell off most of the others to keep the business afloat. One thing for sure, they could never sell the biplane, as she was already getting up in years and could be worth something as a collector's item later.

The sun had not yet evaporated the dew on the fabric as Ana began her preflight inspection.

"Boy, the plane's really wet this morning," she remarked as she inspected the fabric-covered empennage.

"Yeah, if it had been any colder last night it might be frost on those wings. I guess I'll put her inside tonight, just in case." Grant watched her walk around the plane. He was paying attention to two things. One, he ensured she inspected every

seam, bolt, and wire adequately. And two, he observed the way she was put together.

They climbed into the blue and yellow two-holer and cranked her up. For the better part of an hour they put the plane through its paces, sometimes just enjoying the glorious morning. Finally, Grant headed back for the airfield. He had Ana do several landings. She was good and he knew she was ready to solo.

"Pull it over there," he shouted to her as they taxied back after a landing. Ana was a little perplexed. Grant climbed out of the cockpit and stood on the wing next to her.

"This is it," he said, "You're on your own. Take her around the pattern and have a ball. I'll be watching." He tapped her on the head and was gone.

The engine became more faint as he walked back towards the hangar and the house. Then the engine noise built to a crescendo as she roared overhead. Damn, she was good for a student and he knew it. She was good enough to surpass him someday if he didn't take care. He walked out more in the open to watch her fly around the pattern. The beauty of the plane against the morning sky made Grant feel ecstatic. It just doesn't get much better than this, he thought.

He brushed up against something. Looking down, he realized that he had wandered into the flower garden behind the house in his efforts to keep an eye on Ana. It was a rose, a scarlet rose—what an excellent gift for her upon finishing her solo, as well as showing her that he thought she was something special. With his pocket knife, Grant removed the rose with its stem and started for the plane.

Ana taxied the old biplane up to the hangar and spun the tail around in a snappy little turn. The smile on her face said it all. She was proud and downright thrilled with the whole experience. Grant jumped up on the wing and lifted her up in the cockpit. "This rose, Ana, it's for you." The words almost caught in his throat, being so near to her.

"Oh Grant, I'm so happy." She threw her arms around his neck. He swung her to the ground from the wing. Neither one touched the ground as they walked to the hangar.

The following morning Grant met her at the plane with another scarlet rose. Through the days of spring, for as long as the blooms lasted, he gave one to her every time they flew. It became a symbol of their love. A dainty, fragile, yet robust, romance had bloomed.

Eventually, Grant and Ana were married. Their first years were devoted to helping the family flying business to survive. Ana fit well into the scheme of things, as her flying skills were always in demand. Then the war came and Grant went into the

Air Corps. Ana was left behind to tend the business. It was in able hands and, not unexpectedly, the business stayed on course through those uncertain times.

By the late 1950s, however, it became apparent that the small town business would not be enough to support the family. As a matter of necessity, the old grass airport and family homestead was sold. The airplanes that they were using were moved to Chicago and the new hangars, but the old biplane brought a pretty price and was sold as a collector's piece. Essentially, it gave the new business in Chicago its life blood. For the next ten years the business flourished and grew.

At last, time began to take its toll. In any relationship that lasts a lifetime, one of the partners must leave first. In the late 60s, after 35 years of marriage, Ana was struck down by a devastating stroke. Always a fighter, Ana held on for a couple of years, but at last she succumbed to the ailment. Tearfully, Grant faced the future without Ana for the first time in 35 years. Bitter and lonely, it took many months before Grant began to live life again. Even then, Ana was always on his mind.

Ana had been gone for about a year when Grant began looking for a sportplane to help occupy his time. He felt that if he could find an old biplane like he and Ana had flown when they met, he could spend a lot of time rebuilding and flying it to airshows. Word came down through the grapevine that there were a couple of old bipes at an airport a couple hundred miles up-country. Grant took a day to travel there to inspect them.

The airport had all the charm of a country airport. Although the main runway had been paved for some time, there were still a couple of grass strips for crosswind runways. The musky smell of wildflowers and the clang of corrugated metal on the sides of the hangars reminded Grant a great deal of the family's grass airport.

Finally, Grant came across the airport operator. "Say, I heard there were a couple of old ragged biplanes up here for sale. Where might they be?"

"Oh? Well, I didn't know they were for sale, but they are both over there in that row of T-hangars."

"Thanks, I'll be over that way lookin' at them for a while." Grant struck out for the T-hangars. There was a door on the end, through which he entered. It was dark and dank, but he spotted a biplane a few stalls down. Grant stepped back outside and walked over to the hangar doors to see if he could open them and let more light in. He was in luck. The doors were unlocked.

The spring light sprayed into the stall and bathed the old biplane in warmth it hadn't felt in some time. It was in fair shape for such an old plane, Grant thought, but . . . there was the other one a few stalls down. In the dim light it appeared to be painted just like the one he and Ana had owned. Slamming the doors closed on the first hangar, he rushed to the other biplane. It would be great to find an airplane just like the one Ana soloed in. There probably weren't very many left in the world.

Again as the hangar doors moved aside, the old plane was splashed in the morning light. She was blue and yellow and in bad need of dope and fabric. Grant's thoughts began to race. This looks just like our old plane. What was the number we put on her? Darn, I can't remember; it's been so terribly long. She's the right model, though.

He stepped up on the wing and peered into the cockpit hole. The seats looked well-worn. Of course, if this is the same plane, the seats were just about worn out when we sold her.

Grant decided he needed a better look, so he got the airport operator to air the tires and they pushed it out into what was now the afternoon sun. She stood up pert and perky. Even with her tattered and torn fabric she had a contented look, as if reunited with a long-lost friend.

Once again Grant stepped up on the wing. The light was much better now. He looked into the forward cockpit to check its overall condition. Something caught his eye. Reaching down between the seat and the fuselage he retrieved a dried yet preserved scarlet rose. He stared at it for a long time as he held it in both hands, and then began to cry.

"Mister? Are you all right?" The operator was justifiably concerned.

"Yes, I'm all right. I'd explain, but it would take too long." Grant was wondering if the rose had been there for all those years or if it was a sign from Ana.

"Uh," he stopped, trying to collect himself. "Help me push her back into the hangar. I'll come back for this one."

# Rio Gets Even

Life's not all one-sided, as one learns at an early age. There has to be a balance between the good and the bad. At least that's what I tell myself about things like winning and losing.

Mayo is a friend of mine. We instructed together out at the little airport and had fun flying together on occasion. At the time I was just instructing part-time, already being employed at Metro Airlines. Later, Mayo disappeared and I didn't see him for a couple of years. Then one day there he was, walking out to the Rio Twin Otter in a uniform. Then I knew what had happened to Mayo. He had gone to work for the competition. Well, somebody has to fly those yellow planes around.

It became common to run into Mayo around the airports. Occasionally he would ride jump seat in my cockpit and we would talk. After flying for Rio for about two years, Mayo slid into the soft left seat as a captain.

During the years that Mayo was moving up the seniority ladder at Rio, the races went on continuously. If it wasn't my crew, then other Metro crews were busy pitting themselves against the skills of the rival Rio bunch. It was inevitable that Mayo and I would eventually race each other. The only thing is that rarely did either airline know who was in the other airplane.

The last flight at night back to Wichita Falls from DFW is always the most-raced flight segment of the day. The reason is really simple and not actually competitive at all. The earlier a flight crew gets in, the earlier they get to go home or drink a beer or whatever. This coupled with the fact that Rio and Metro flights are often scheduled to leave at the same time, makes a race just an added incentive.

Rio's passenger loading is straightforward. The passengers walk from the terminal to the airplane. At Metro it is different. In fact, it stinks. Our passengers are brought from the center of the terminal on little shuttle buses and that usually means we leave the gate much after Rio. Sometimes the difference in time is over ten minutes.

Luckily, this often has a hidden advantage. Since many Rio flights and several American flights leave at the same time, plus a couple of Metro flights, the runways are crowded for departure. As a result, the Wichita Falls-bound flight has to taxi to the far west side of the airport for departure. If Metro is slow getting out of the gate, we often have the advantage of most departures being gone and thus get the near east side runway. We make up a few minutes on Rio by that break alone.

Metro also has another advantage and hence an equalizer, a faster airplane. Our Shorts SD3-30 (which is no longer on the route, but was at the time of this race) is about 30 knots faster. Thus, an airborne head start of five to seven minutes makes the race between Twin Otter and Shorts a pretty fair race over the 100-mile-long course.

As usual, Rio was out of the blocks well ahead of us. They probably left the ramp a good ten minutes before we had our people boarded. We put a fire in the holes and taxied out. Rio's strobe was twinkling in the sky as they turned westward. We were still on the ramp. The time between us would be about seven minutes if we got the near runway. We did.

Things were working in our favor that night. At least the timing was good for a fair race. The glare of the Fort Worth metropolitan area hid the strobes on Rio's plane. They were camouflaged among the stars, the DFW inbounds, and the glary haze. Out there ahead of us and unseen for now, we couldn't really know what altitude they were choosing to use. We chose 8,500 feet to take advantage of two factors. For one thing, we could take advantage of a higher true airspeed than at 6,500. Also Rio had a habit of not flying any higher than 6,500 westbound. At 8,500 feet we'd probably be above them and could take advantage of that extra stored energy. The plan was to change that altitude into airspeed and that's where we had them. The Shorts redline is a great deal higher than the Otter's.

Away from the city lights, we laid eyes on Rio making a beeline for the Falls. Sure enough, they were below us and we were holding our own "distance-wise" as we continued the climb. The visibility in this part of the country is normally excellent; 50 miles is the norm and 80 to 100 is not rare. We could see the Falls as well as we could see Rio and that helped. Picking our own best direct line to the airport helped cut the distance we had to fly to the minimum.

One of the benefits to being behind in a race of this nature is that the competition has no idea where you are. They don't know how close you're following or when to pick the best time to start descending. If your plane is fast enough, all the advantages lie with the trailing airplane.

The flight between DFW and SPS (Wichita Falls) goes by fast in any airplane. Even in an Otter the flight is only 45 minutes. That doesn't leave much time to maneuver for position. As we scooted along, we slowly gained on Rio. At last it was time to descend. All the stored energy was converted to airspeed and we slid by the Twin Otter in the dark easily. The airport was close to both airplanes and Approach Control had us first for the runway—but not by much.

Unknown to me, at the time, Mayo was flying as the Rio captain. No slouch as an aviator, he planned his own strategy to beat us to the terminal. There are three runways at Shepherd Air Force Base on which Mayo could choose to land. Runway 35 is closest to the civil ramp and we were lined up to land on it. Mayo chose to follow us as closely as he could and play the airplane characteristics of the Otter against those of the Shorts—a wise move indeed.

The Otter can land short and a Shorts, ironically, cannot. We touched down doing about 110 knots. The rollout was long and Mayo was right on our tails. The controller instructed us to roll out and take the mid-field taxiway.

"Uh-oh, that's trouble for us," I remarked to my copilot. We had to taxi fast if we were to beat them to the ramp.

Rio touched down and stopped in about a thousand feet. "Rio, make a 180 and turn left at the end," the controller instructed.

"Roger," Mayo answered, and I recognized his voice. The Otter turned around and sped for the end. We had to slow for a turn prior to reaching the runway, but we'd catch them dead even at the turn to the terminal. Our fate, after a hard-fought race, was now in the ground controller's hands.

"Metro, hold short of the runway; give way to Rio and follow him to the ramp." The words cut like a knife. After our hard-won lead, it was not to be. Mayo zipped around the corner in front of us.

I said "Shucks"—or something like that—and keyed the microphone. I was talking to the controller: "You know you just cost me five dollars by letting Rio in front of us."

"Well, gee, I'm sorry. I didn't know it was that important," the controller jibed back.

Then Mayo came on: "That's all right. We think you do great work. And I'll split the five bucks with you." Then there was a reflective pause and he added, "If I can collect it."

# All Hung Up

Some guys and gals are addicted to it. They try it once and they are hooked. My opinion doesn't account for much, but they have got to be flaky. I mean, anyone who jumps out of a perfectly good airplane can't have all his/her marbles. Or maybe they've just all rolled to one side.

Being in aviation professionally, one comes across these characters on occasion. They are different from normal human beings. It's probably because they live life all the time on the ragged edge. A string of vitality runs their being that most of us don't have. That's all right with me, though. If it takes jumping out of an airplane to be blessed with that fiber of vitality, I'll remain content to walk the Earth without that extra spring in my step.

The plane was a Cessna 206. It's a good jump plane because of the removable cargo doors on the right side of the fuselage. With the doors removed, the hole is large and behind the wing for the most part. Jumping out the doors is as easy as falling off a log. The only trouble is that the log is thousands of feet in the air.

Perfect jump days only come along occasionally. A perfect day is not just a blue sky and good visibility. For a jumper, the temperature has to be just right, with light winds, and most of all good friends. When all these factors get together, then that's a perfect day to jump. Today was perfect.

Katrina Stevens, called Katt by her friends, was about to make her third jump. All night long she had been hardly able to sleep with the anticipation of today's jump. It might be just a static line jump, but it still held the greatest excitement for her. As she walked to the plane with her gear, she said a quiet prayer under her breath. This sport might be as safe as they say, but we can all use a little help, she figured.

Several other static line jumpers were aboard the flight, and one fellow was going up a little higher than the rest to do a free fall. As the assortment of highly individualistic individuals crawled into the airplane's rear cavity they mimicked each other. A couple of them grabbed Katt and threw her in, shouting something about her body was theirs if she could catch them. Like I said, these people like to have fun—and why not? They never know if this will be the last time they walk on Earth with all their parts intact.

Katt was first to go out. The pilot maneuvered the plane over the drop zone according to the jumpmaster's instructions: "Five degrees left; five more left," Dave yelled to Chris, who was deftly spotting the plane in the blind from Dave's instructions. Katt began to make her way out the door. Gingerly, she stepped onto the right main tire and held on to the wing strut. She waited for the engine to be cut and the signal from her instructor.

She was watching below, anxious for the engine to be cut. Apprehensive, nervous, and a little shaky, she hadn't quite gotten into the routine of all this. Wham! The air filled with the sound of snapping nylon. Then she felt a terrible jerk. Looking above to see if the canopy had opened, Katt stared into a clear, ice-blue sky. The chute had opened prematurely while she was standing on the tire. A glance at her altimeter on the reserve pack showed her not to be descending. "What the . . . ," she muttered to herself. Then she realized, "My God, I'm hung on the tail!"

The stark reality of the situation hit Katt like a dynamite explosion. In essence, she was trapped and there wasn't any way to ask anyone for help. Whatever she did would have to be her own idea.

Inside the 206 the action was frantic. The pilot found it necessary to handle the airplane with both hands and they were losing altitude at a rate of 300 feet per minute. Above the screaming engine the jumpmaster called to the pilot: "You want me to get these guys out?"

"Yeah, and hurry!" he shouted back.

With that, Dave hooked the other two up on quickly rigged static lines. Safety dictated the jumpers go out and on a static line at this point due to their altitude (below 3,000 feet above the ground). Out they went, filing by Katt on the way.

Katt watched them sail by. She thought, "Maybe they don't know I'm back here. Or, worse yet, maybe they think the plane is going to crash soon and they aren't going to be on it when it does." That last thought sobered Katt greatly. The wind was beating her unmercifully and the shroud lines were beginning to twist as she rolled over and over in the wind. Above, she could barely hear the engine wailing against gravity and its unconventional load.

"I've got to cut away," Katt began talking to herself. It was to keep herself calm and assure she did everything right. After all, she had no practice at this sort of thing. "After I get the shroud lines loose I'm going to count to three and pull my reserve.

117

God, I hope *it* works!" Reaching down was no easy proposition, all hung up the way she was. Cautiously, she grasped the knife in the scabbard on her right leg.

"Boy, if I drop this thing I've had it." A cold sweat began to develop as she lifted the knife from the leather sheath. It's funny, she thought, that she should start sweating now. Holding the knife ever so tightly, she cut the twisted lines on her right shoulder. She began to swing a little more freely in the torrent of air.

"Get my left side and it's one, two, three, pull. It better work." The knife sliced through about half the lines. Katt closed her eyes as she drew the knife across them one more time. She was free.

"One, two, three!" Katt screamed as she pulled the ring on the reserve. The nylon slapped the air and gave a firm, reassuring tug as the canopy opened above. "Thank you, God. Thank you," she whispered.

In the airplane, the situation improved only slightly when Katt cut loose. The parachute quickly blew off the horizontal stabilizer, but the stabilizer was damaged. The airplane rocked and bucked as the engine struggled with its injury. Dave, the jumpmaster, looked at his altimeter—2,500 feet. If he was going to leave he had better get along. He motioned to Chris that he was leaving. Hooking up a static line as he had done for the others, he bailed out.

Chris was thinking seriously of going with him. He reached down and felt the loose crotch straps. There was no way he could hook up now. The airplane required two hands and that's all there was to it. It looked like he and the 206 were partners for better or for worse.

The airplane heaved and bucked as Chris maneuvered for his final approach. He was hoping dearly that it wasn't really *his final approach*. The airspeed stayed up around 110 miles per hour. That is a little fast for a 206, but he didn't know what the plane would do at a lower speed. There was so little back elevator left. If he could just drive it on with no flare, the odds for success were the greatest. At 110 mph the wheels screeched against the runway. Chris yanked the throttle back. If she porpoises, he thought, I'm going to ride her till she stops. It was obvious. There was no way to go around.

The plane streaked down the runway in a well-behaved manner. Eventually the brakes did their job and stopped all the excitement. Chris breathed a sigh of relief as he taxied his wounded bird to the ramp. A crowd of skydivers surrounded the plane as soon as the prop stopped.

An inspection showed that the elevator had been jammed by a severely bent and torn right horizontal stabilizer—an unaerodynamic-looking mess to be sure. Then Chris thought about Katt. "Where's Katt?"

An anonymous voice filled him in: "Oh, she's on her way in. Harold had to go over to the other side of the field to get her. She's all right I think; here she comes now."

Chris continued the conversation, "Did everyone else get down okay?" About that time Katt came walking up. She still looked a little pale.

The skydiver continued speaking as he watched Katt walk into the group. "Well, everyone got down okay except Charlie. He got hung up on a power pole. I guess a lot of us have been hung up around here today," he chided. "Huh, Katt?"

# Dim Wit

By now we have established two things in the pages of this book. One is that flying mail in the Pacific Northwest was a demanding and often frightful job. The second is that Aztec 56 Yankee was a dog of an airplane. The tricks that airplane could pull never seemed to end. That was the reason for my nightly psyching process before work. One couldn't just go to work casually; that would be dangerous. I had to be fired up and ready to handle anything that old dog would throw at me. And believe me, she could throw the best.

It was my last night to fly the trip down to Boise—a fine time for a dirty trick. The flight to Boise from Lewiston was uneventful, as it normally was. I have often wondered why 56Y would always show her peculiar qualities on the northbound flights. The truth, it seems, is that she must have had to warm up, like an old tube-type radio. After all, she *was* about that vintage.

The Hell's Canyon area of Oregon at night seems to be a mysterious and forboding place. The night sky above is every bit as dangerous as the river that rages in the chasm below. Most nights you can't even see the Seven Devils cloaked in their cape of white. And then, some nights the mountains reach up out of that milky chowder like the teeth of a great shark seemingly bent on ripping planes from the sky. It's a toss-up as to which condition is more frightening—the not-seeing-yet-knowing-they-are-there, or facing those cavity-pitted teeth just under the belly.

Limitations are what kept the Aztec in close proximity to the hills. She just could not climb or fly much higher. Even the jets, though, occasionally had problems transiting the canyon. One particular evening as we flew southbound towards Boise, 56Y began to lose altitude. All instruments indicated that everything was normal. It had to be a downdraft.

Since we were at MEA (2,000 feet AGL), it didn't take much altitude loss to instill a great deal of worry, and 56Y was slipping further into the hole despite increases to full power. My pucker factor increased in proportion to how low we descended. Finally, after losing 750 feet, she began a slow climb back to altitude.

I passed along the word of the downdraft to the controller. He already knew about it, and said that even the big boys had been reporting a strong downdraft at 35,000 feet in the exact same spot. The weather happened to be clear that night, so what was it? Not being superstitious, but imaginative, I blamed it on a great whirlpool over Hell's Canyon funneling us seafarers of the air into its darkest depths. The canyon affects everyone who treads there. It's magically ominous, destructive, and impossible to ignore.

After filling the plane with mail and fuel for the last air mail flying I'd ever do, we said goodbye to the Boise controllers and headed north. At 10,000 feet the glow of Boise disappeared behind us as we poked our nose into the clouds and the Salmon River Canyon. The disc jockey on KOB in Albuquerque was playing all my favorite Country-and-Western favorites and I was quite relaxed as the plane hummed towards Hell's Canyon. All the previous anxieties that I had shared with 56Y in the past were forgotten for now. One more trip across the "big ditch" and I would be a veteran.

Hell's Canyon had thrown just about everything at me in the past; I thought there was nothing left. That was an unwise assumption.

Have you ever given any thought to what you should do in the event of complete electrical failure while the plane is solid IFR? If you haven't, you really should. In certain meteorological conditions and geographical locations, the options are usually few. Maybe there are really no safe ones at all. In the western mountain states or eastern mountainous areas, descending without radio guidance may be suicidal. The experts—meaning the FAA—say that a pilot should fly his planned route and descend in VFR conditions or fly to the nearest VFR conditions. At that point, one's heading and time-distance computations take on great importance.

Those are great logical ideas, but there is one condition they don't address. If all the cloud bases are below your last cleared altitude and there are mountains of various elevations in all directions, then where do you let down? Luck and prayer—not necessarily in that order—will determine the success of the descent.

I was as unprepared for electrical failure as the next guy. As 56Y droned over the canyon we were handed off to Seattle center. Our descent clearance followed and we started down, still in the clouds. The panel lights seemed to be getting dimmer. Unconsciously, I reached down and turned the knob to brighten them. A few minutes went by before there were any more exchanges on the radio.

"Great Western 612, you're now cleared to . . . thousand."
The controller's voice seemed to trail away.

"Say again for Great Western 612." The reply was weaker
than the last, but I pulled 8,000 out of it as my suspicions became
aroused. The panel lights became even more dim. Once again I
turned them up and began to ponder the problem.

At first I was thankful that we had received the clearance to
8,000 feet. Experience had taught me that seldom were the cloud
bases below that level. But what if they weren't? What if the next
transmission from center was too weak to read, or I didn't hear it
at all? Why were the lights getting so dim?

Logically, I should have devoted the most thought to solving
the electrical problem first. However, I chose to develop a plan of
action if I was caught in the clouds. It only takes the brain a
second and then one has the remainder of his time for the
mechanics of the situation.

Here was my plan: I would continue the heading toward the
Pullman VORTAC. That heading would take me directly over
Lewiston. The clouds would light up over the city, so I would
know when I was over the town. Then I would fly for five more
minutes, which would put me in the vicinity of the VORTAC. The
terrain around the VORTAC is gently rolling, with no
mountains for many miles in a northerly direction. I could let
down to 4,000 feet there and not hit anything—and more than
likely be VFR.

With a sure-fire plan in my mind, I began to devote attention
to the electrical problem. The VOR needle oscillated back and
forth like a windshield wiper and rolled over dead. That was it.
Things were going to hell fast even though most accessory
equipment had been turned off already.

"Great Western 612." The controller's voice was faint.
"Descend to 4,000 if Lewiston is not in sight; you are cleared for
an approach."

"Great Western 612, down to four now and cleared for an
approach."

"Great Western, you radio . . ." His voice trailed off. That
was all I heard. Out of 7,000 feet the city of Lewiston appeared. It
was a golden sight. I reported that I had the airport in sight for a
visual. There was no response; 56Y and I were safe—no thanks to
her.

Further investigation showed that both generators had
kicked off the line. I reset the breakers and we flew on in. Relieved
to be on the ground, I made a mistake and shut down both
engines. After unloading the mail, the engines would not start
due to low voltage on the battery. At 2:00 A.M. there is no one who
is going to give a plane an APU boost in Lewiston, Idaho. The

rest of the mail was trucked to Spokane that night and I spent the night in the mail carrier's basement.

The plan for a descent from 8,000 feet would have worked and been safe, I am sure. But an electrical failure in IFR conditions can hardly be planned for. One never knows where one will be when it happens. With 56 Yankee, though, you always knew where she'd stab you in the back—right over Hell's Canyon.

# If at First You Don't Succeed . . .

The weather was stifling the best efforts of pilots throughout Texas. It was a spring night, and virtually all of Texas east of the Pecos was being drowned.

Phil Schubert was spending his time alternately between the window in the terminal and the phone to Flight Service. The window provided a good look at the way the weather looked everywhere that night. Rain drummed down on the Beech 99 outside as if it might not stop for 40 days.

As Phil looked out on the ramp, another plane came splashing up. Its taxi light fell on the puddles being bombarded by millions of silver drops. Entranced by the sight, Phil continued staring out the window until the props turned to a stop. A lightning flash lit the ramp as the crew dashed across to the terminal. It was bright enough that Phil recognized them as a crew that came from down south, the direction he needed to go. He made his way down the steps to the crew room to get a first-hand pilot report. As Phil pushed the door open, the lately arrived captain turned to see who it was. Water was still dripping off his hat.

"Well, look who's here—Phil Schubert. I thought you'd be out there sloshing through the sky somewhere." He had a broad smile.

"How's it going, Jim?"

"Oh, not too bad. A little wet though, huh?"

"Sure is," Phil replied. "How was your ride coming north?"

"Not too bad. A little bumpy, though. Lots of lightning. A hell of a lot of lightning, come to think of it."

"Would you go back through it?" Phil asked the definitive question. Sometimes that's the only way a guy can get to the truth. Some pilots are just too macho to admit the trip scared them out of ten years of life.

"Oh yeah. Definitely." Jim was emphatic. He knew his credibility was being measured.

It was the answer that Phil was looking for. "Then I guess

we'll try it if they'll let us out of here. Last time I talked to them they weren't letting any departures out."

"Well, good luck with it," the captain said, and returned to his paperwork.

"Yeah, we'll see ya around." Phil walked back upstairs to notify the ticket agents of his decision to leave. As usual, they were incredibly happy to get a few demanding passengers off their hands.

They loaded the plane with the few passengers who had hung around after the flight had been delayed indefinitely for weather. Phil and his copilot got both props turning and taxied out. The airport was deserted of other traffic. Fort Worth Center was holding all high traffic departures, but the low ones could get out.

Once airborne, Phil requested 4,000 feet to College Station. Jim had been right—it was bumpy and there was lots of lightning. Phil turned the panel lights up and lowered his seat to avoid the brunt of the flashes.

The flight to College Station was your average bumpy flight. Controlling the plane was a full-time job and the crew would be happy to shoot the approach and land. As the flight progressed, however, the weather in the College Station area took a turn for the worse.

Phil's wife Diane was home watching television, waiting for the time to go to the airport and pick him up. A bulletin was issued. There were tornadoes reported in the area and everyone was told to take shelter. The nearest public shelter was the airport, so Diane left home for there.

Cleared for the approach, Phil got the 99 headed outbound for the procedure turn. As they crossed the outer marker outbound, the air became smooth as glass. It was a little spooky. Turning around, they crossed the outer marker again and the bouncing started again. The runway came into sight early. The approach was going to be a cinch. It *was* a cinch until decision height. Then the runway and lights disappeared and water pounded the windshield like someone had turned on a fire hose.

"Missed approach!" Phil called as he began the missed approach procedure. The crew began cleaning the airplane up for another go at it. All of a sudden, the cockpit was filled with the clang of the fire bell. The right engine fire warning was illuminated. The copilot reached to pull the emergency handle.

"Don't pull it!" Phil commanded. "With all that water, I don't see how we could have a fire. It's probably a short in the fire detection loop."

As the plane turned downwind, they saw the runway again. Quickly they requested a contact approach. Obviously, they could land this time. The plane swung over the approach lights, and again everything went dark outside. Part of the storm was stationed right at the end of the runway.

"We're going around again!" Phil was becoming exasperated.

Diane was just entering the terminal as the 99 made its second pass overhead. There were two older women inside mopping the floor. One turned to the other as Diane walked towards them.

"I don't think he's gonna make it. It's a-blowin' too hard."

"Oh yeah. He'll make it." the other one said.

"Lawdy, honey, I don't see how he's gonna land out there in that mess," the discussion continued.

As Diane was about to open her mouth to speak to the two women, the door to the ramp swung wide open and the janitor walked in from outside.

"Have you seen my husband? He's usually here by now." Wives have a way of not understanding weather and the implications it holds for their pilot husbands. The janitor pointed upwards, meaning that Phil was somewhere overhead.

The debate between the two cleaning women went on. "Honey, he's done been down the runway and didn't land. He's not gonna make it."

"Oh yeah, he'll keep right on till he gets that ol' airplane down."

Up above, Phil was beginning to wonder if he'd get the plane down in one piece. If the weather and fire light were not enough problems to handle, then the nacelle fuel-low light that just came on was.

"Easterwood Tower, what's your wind now?" Phil was thinking of using a different runway.

"It's 100 at 10 gusting to 18."

"How about runway 10 for landing?"

"You're cleared to land any runway you like."

"Okay, then, we'll land 10." There was determination in his voice. Lined up for the runway, the entire airport was becoming blurred by sheets of rain. Phil hung with it. He lost the lights for a second or two, but just kept the runway heading, feeling his way down. At long last, there was a splash as the plane touched solid—but wet—ground. The rain increased in intensity and the taxi to the terminal took a good five minutes. For 10 or 15 minutes afterward the passengers and crew sat on the ramp inside the plane, being rocked by the wind. Eventually the storm moved off and everyone dashed for the terminal.

As Phil walked towards Diane, one of the cleaning ladies spoke to her. "See, I told ya he'd make it."

127

Phil looked at Diane. "What's that all about?"

"C'mon, let's go home," she said, "I'll tell you about it on the way."

"All right with me. And boy, do I have a story tell you!"

# Is the Customer *Always* Right?

Upstate New York is beautiful in the summer. The tree-covered slopes of the Catskills and Adirondacks flow from peak to valley like a great emerald ocean. What way is more glorious to view the sight than from the quiet perch of a glider soaring the currents high above? Probably none—at least that is what Don Wright's boss thought when he bought three Schweizer 233s for tourist rides. Don got the job flying the sailplanes during summer vacation from college. It was a great way to earn money, build time, and gain experience—15 to 20 minutes at a clip.

The business of giving rides was lucrative. Tourist season in the mountains is almost always good; weekends are even better. They could keep all three planes in the air on almost any day during the summer. At $15 a ride, the business was making money and so were the pilots.

Occasionally, they really earned their money.

Don had been watching the clouds since late morning. From 10:00 on they had looked like big heads of cauliflower. It wouldn't surprise him if they went to thundering at any time. As he returned to the field, the towering Cu to the southwest had just started to show a rain shaft underneath. It was maturing. He coasted to his place in line—third. A line of prospective passengers had appeared at around 11:00 and business had been steady since. It looked for all the world like the rest of the afternoon would be just as profitable.

One after another the sailplanes were tethered to the towplane and pulled aloft until Don was next in line. The little buildup was now a full-fledged thunderstorm and just about to reach the field. His boss, being a businessman, urged him to take off and make the flight.

"Oh, I think it'll be all right, Don. At least you can get this one out of the way before the rain."

"Well, maybe. I'll give it a try at least. If it's all right with you." Don turned to his passenger.

"Sure, heck yeah! If you'll go, I'll go," the man said. Don wondered how many times he'd heard that from passengers. I suppose it's their way of building their confidence and keeping their nerve, he thought.

Soon they were airborne. Don could hear the little Decathlon laboring to pull both planes skyward. The storm was looking darker and occasionally both airplanes would take a pretty good jolt. The tow pilot was getting nervous about it with two airplanes in such close proximity to each other and the storm. He gave Don the signal to release. Don pulled the handle and pulled the stick back and to the right. The towplane disappeared down and to the left.

The storm seized the glider like an iron fist. The updraft pushed them upward at an incredible rate. Don extended the spoilers and full dive brakes. Still the sailplane climbed—tail first. It was no use; they climbed upward at over 2,000 feet per minute. Don's passenger was excited. "Hey, this is great. Boy, this glider really goes!"

Don could scarcely believe what he was hearing. There they were in the grip of a storm, not even knowing if the plane would hold together, and this guy was having fun. All some people know about planes is that they fly. Like everything goes up, they must eventually come down.

At the base of the storm cloud they hit the downdraft. The vertical speed indicator now showed 2,000 feet per minute down. It was now possible for Don to get a little forward momentum and fly slowly away from the storm. Monstrous though it was, the storm released its death grip on the little glider. Don headed straight for the airport.

Racing anything but another glider in a glider is nearly futile. Nonetheless, they raced for the airport, trying to beat the storm. Don hit the taxiway at a gallop and coasted across the field for the hangar. Several ground handlers grabbed the wings and pushed the sailplane in the hangar as the rain began to come down in sheets.

Don pushed the canopy open once inside the hangar. Looking at his watch, he noted that the whole flight had only taken about eight minutes. It seemed to him he had lived a lifetime in the jaws of the storm. Then came the clincher.

"Say, I thought you said the ride would take 15 to 20 minutes?" the passenger demanded.

Don wasn't one to mince words. "Friend, that was the ride of a lifetime and the only one like it I want to make in *this* lifetime. If it wasn't enough for you, talk to the boss." With that, Don strode across the hangar and disappeared.

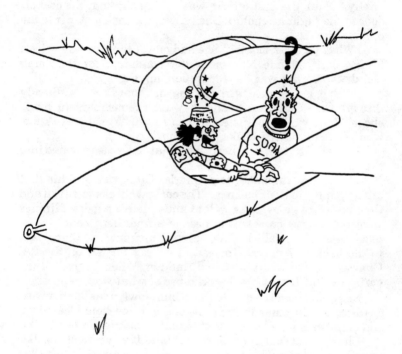

# That's One Way to Do It

"Kelly." Paul, the first officer, was calling through the cockpit door to the flight attendant. She turned and took a step into the cockpit.

"What ya need, sugar?" She had one of those cutesy voices. Fluffy, curly blonde hair made her candidate for the dumb blonde type. That was her reputation, anyway.

"We've got a deaf girl coming on board. She's already through the ticket counter and they don't remember which one she is," Paul explained. Then, he continued, "You have to know who she is for safety's sake, don't you?"

"Sure do. But I'll find her." With that Kelly disappeared into the cabin.

In the meantime, Captain Charles Kilpatrick and his first officer tended to their business. The cockpit checks were run and they began to go over the weight-and-balance papers. Minutes went by and the crew was in need of a final head count in the passenger cabin. Kelly had not yet come up front, and the curtain to the back was closed. Instead of calling for her on the PA, Charles decided to go back and find her. When he pushed the curtain aside, he got his first glimpse of what was going on.

Kelly was near the rear of the cabin, slowly making her way forward. As she came to each row of seats, she would lean over and clap her hands behind each female passenger's head.

Charles just couldn't believe the sight. It was ridiculous, like something out of a Three Stooges movie. He walked up to Kelly, shaking his head.

"Kelly, what are you doing?"

"I'm looking for the deaf girl. If she doesn't turn around when I clap, I'll know she's deaf. Don't you remember telling me to find her?" Kelly looked so innocent and naive.

"Of course, darling, but don't you think you could make an announcement and ask everyone who hears you to raise his hand? Then, when the deaf girl doesn't raise her hand, you'd know."

Kelly reflected for a moment. Then in a sheepish voice that sounded like one of those blonde bombshells on *Hee Haw,* she answered.

"Gee, yeah. I never thought of that. You're so smart. I guess that's why you're the Captain!"

"Well, maybe," said Charles with a smile. Then he turned around and started back toward the cockpit, counting heads as he went. He didn't want to know what her method for counting passengers might be.

# Benoit's Crash*

Here's an ag flying story that's worth retelling. Gordon Baxter wrote it up for his column "Bax 'N Forth" in *Ag Pilot International* magazine.

Benoit (pronounced ben-wah) went into the woods loaded. His 450 P&W quit cold while his high-lift Stearman was low and slow over the woods—those scraggly hardwoods that grow in the wooded swamps around some of the rice fields. Benoit walked away from it. Or I should say waded.

I always wanted to ask some guy who'd done it what it was like. So, after a decent interval, I asked him.

"Did you find a little clearing? Or did you find a pair of trees you could shed the wings on? What were you thinking?"

"All I was thinking, Bax, was that I was going to be shaking hands with all the hookers in Hell in a minute."

He never did tell me anything about the crash. I don't think he can. But he told me a lot about what all happened right after the crash.

"I got out and stepped off the lower left wing root and into cold black water about up to my waist. My wingman was circling over me, looking. I waved at him, he waved back, then he waggled his wings and pointed and took up a heading toward the nearest clearing and high ground. He knew what I needed."

Benoit says he never looked back at what was left of the plane. "I could hear those alligators barking."

I don't think alligators bark, but it's Benoit's crash and he can tell it any way he wants to. He says he made it out of the swamp in no time.

"I made it out into the sunlight and up onto a rice levee, the woods behind me, looking out over the field we had been working. It was going to be a long walk."

Benoit's outfit flew all Stearmans in those days. Immaculate planes. The company had a shop that did it all but engine majors. They had a wing room and fuselage jigs, and still had lots of cherry PT-13s stacked for parts. They could bring in a crash that made just about a pickup truck load and have it flying again in a few weeks if the season was on and they'd already used up their reserves. Belly-ups and torn-up wing bays they could just about do overnight. The only bad jobs were if the frame got bent, and it took a lot to bend a Stearman frame.

Benoit said, "I'd no sooner got out in the clear and here came a herd of our loader trucks and jeeps and pickups across the rice field. They had called each other up by radio, they were jumping levees, guys hanging onto the outside, it looked like a John Wayne movie. I thought, 'Those guys really care about me.'"

Benoit says they went tearing right on by, never slowed down. He says one of them leaned out and yelled, *"Did you bend the frame?"*

*By Gordon Baxter, ©1983 *Ag Pilot International.* Reprinted with the kind permission of Tom J. Wood.

# Different Strokes

There are two kinds of pilots: Civilian and Military. And there are two kinds of military pilots: Fighter Pilots and Others.

The fighter pilots, who fly the world's most sophisticated, advanced, and high-performance machinery, look upon themselves as a breed apart—and rightly so. They take no small pleasure in ribbing the bomber, tanker, and transport drivers, who have to bravely grin and bear the abuse—right up until the day when they get to list all that lovely multi-engine jet time on their commercial airline job application forms. Walk into any saloon that caters to the GI flier trade and you'll find the fighter jocks at one end of the bar, yukking it up and gesturing wildly with flattened hands, the universal sign language of the tiger. (It has been said that if you tied a fighter pilot's hands behind his back, he'd be unable to utter a single word.) The many-motored crews are at the other end of the bar—or, more likely, in booths—quietly discussing the finer points of interest rates, stock margins, and property values.

Every now and then, though, one of the "big guys" gets the last word. This story has been told and retold so many times in so many ways that it's probably apocryphal by now, but, like all good hangar tales, *something like it* probably happened *sometime, somewhere.*

It was at the height of the late unpleasantness in Southeast Asia, and an Air National Guard unit was spending their annual two-week "summer camp" flying American wounded back to the States in their medivac-equipped C-121s. (In case you're not up on military designations, the C-121 is the graceful old Lockheed Constellation, which dates back to 1943.) One of the "Connies" had just left Saigon and was heading for Hawaii when it picked up an escort—a pair of F-4D Phantom fighters.

One of the Phantom jocks came up on the radio: "Hey, Connie, that sure is a beautiful bird."

"Uh, roger, thanks," responded the Guard pilot.

"Yeah, it sure brings a tear of nostalgia to my eye. That

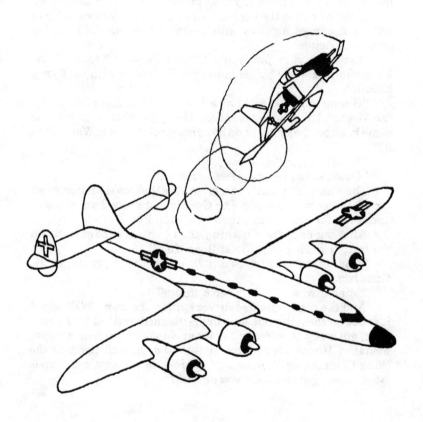

three-tailer is still pretty after all these years," said the jock, referring to the aging Guard machine.

The Guard pilot detected just a hint of sarcasm in the compliment. "Yeah, it sure does beat that cobbled-up looking piece of trash you're saddled with. That thing looks like a model put together by a kid who read all the instructions backward."

"Ah, yes, my friend," rejoindered the jock, in his best W. C. Fields impression, "but beauty is in the eye of the beholder, form follows function, and pretty is as pretty does. Watch this." And so saying, he pulled the big F-4 up into a series of vertical aileron rolls that caused an involuntary radio transmission from his own back-seater.

"Let's see your pretty old Connie do *that*," taunted the Phantom jock as he pulled back into formation with the flying hospital.

"Gimme a break; you know I can't do anything like that," the Weekend Warrior responded. Then, pausing a minute, he came back on the radio: "I do have one trick, though. Want to see it?"

"By all means," said the jock.

"Okay, stand by one. Here it comes."

The Phantom pulled out a bit to give the Constellation room for whatever was coming. The Connie just droned on, straight and level, for one minute, then two, then five.

After ten minutes of nothing, the Phantom pilot came up on the box: "Hey, big guy, I'm still waiting."

"You mean you missed it?" came the reply from the Guardsman.

"Missed what? I didn't see a thing."

And the many-motored driver sprung the trap: "Well, son, I just put on the autopilot, stood up, stretched, walked back to the john, got a cup of coffee and a donut, shook hands with a future Medal of Honor winner, got invited to a cocktail party at the Wing Commander's house, and made a date with a cute nurse. Now, smart guy, *let's see you do that!*"

# Too Close for Comfort

Most Sundays are laid-back, but everything about this Sunday was special from the instant I opened my eyes. I was in high anticipation of making my second supervised solo. All sorts of anxieties were on my mind as I mentally prepared for the moment I knew would come when I would hold my own destiny in my hand. Would it be too gusty? Would I get airborne before the hot afternoon thermals built up to jostle my landings around?

As I arrived at the old blue terminal building, I could see the local skydiving freaks repacking their chutes before a gaggle of admiring young ladies and preparing to take another 7,500-foot plunge. The jump plane pilot had his hands full as he determinedly tried to coax life into the big round 300 Lycoming on his faded Cessna 190.

I walked inside and signed for a Cessna 150. Dave, my instructor, was grinning his challenge and asking if I was ready to fly. I said I was as ready as I would ever be and grinned back.

After preflighting the little yellow and white Cessna, we got off to a good start. Dave kept leaning over into my ear, making suggestions to improve my fledgling technique while the plane went around the pattern doing touch-and-goes. Then he said, "Let me out and be careful." The moment was at hand. I taxied back to the terminal and let Dave out, taking care not to disturb the bright and newly folded canopies of the chute packers with my prop blast. Then the little Cessna and I headed out to share the sky alone.

The first landing was a little bumpy. Another try was in order to clean up the record. On the Unicom I could hear the big blind 190 calling for an Airport Advisory prior to taxiing with his load of "death wish" jumpers. The next landing proved that I was beginning to master the little plane, so I poured on the power for another try. I felt as good as I could feel.

Somewhere behind me as I turned the 150 to the downwind leg for runway 30, the jump plane took off. I reported the customary downwind position and began a turn to base leg when

139

I heard those chilling words: "Beaumont! Emergency! Landing runway one two!" Boy, someone was in trouble. I craned around to see while turning final for three zero.

Then it hit me! "Runway 12! Good God, that's the other end of *my* runway." For an instant I just sat there, searching the pattern for that other plane. Then I heard Dave's voice on the radio. "Jeff, make a 360 to the right." There wasn't even time enough to call the aircraft tail number. I broke right, staring down into the big window of the tower. I could see Dave gripping the mike as I roared overhead, still blind to whatever the danger was. There was something in the setup that just didn't seem kosher and I decided not to make a complete 360 degree turn. I just firewalled the throttle and hauled it up and away from the pattern for all she'd take. That instinct saved my life and a load of jumpers too.

The big Cessna 190 had blown a jug after takeoff and made a 180 trying to get back to the runway. He made it easily, but went too far. He was too high and hot. It bounced down the active, sliced the piece of air I would have been in, pulled up into a stall over the highway and power lines, and smashed into a field, totalled. Fortunately, all the jumpers were out and running.

On that particular day I became enlightened to one of the most elemental facts of flying. It has paid many, many dividends since. A pilot must be prepared for any eventuality. If my instructor hadn't warned me, I'd have met that old round-faced Cessna head-on. And if I'd gone around in a 360, we would have cut each other in two.

On the lighter side, I have the dubious reputation and distinction of being the ony student in history to buzz the tower on his second supervised solo while looking his instructor right in the eye.